Blood on Their Hands

Blood on Their Hands

Japanese Military Atrocities 1931–1945

Cecil Lowry

Pen & Sword
MILITARY

First published in Great Britain in 2024 by
Pen & Sword Military
An imprint of Pen & Sword Books Limited
Yorkshire – Philadelphia

ISBN 978 1 39903 787 7

A CIP catalogue record for this book is
available from the British Library.

Typeset by Mac Style
Printed in the UK by CPI Group (UK) Ltd, Croydon, CR0 4YY.

MIX
Paper | Supporting responsible forestry
FSC® C013604

Pen & Sword Books Limited incorporates the imprints of After the Battle, Atlas, Archaeology, Aviation, Discovery, Family History, Fiction, History, Maritime, Military, Military Classics, Politics, Select, Transport, True Crime, Air World, Frontline Publishing, Leo Cooper, Remember When, Seaforth Publishing, The Praetorian Press, Wharncliffe Local History, Wharncliffe Transport, Wharncliffe True Crime and White Owl.

For a complete list of Pen & Sword titles please contact

PEN & SWORD BOOKS LIMITED
47 Church Street, Barnsley, South Yorkshire, S70 2AS, England
E-mail: enquiries@pen-and-sword.co.uk
Website: www.pen-and-sword.co.uk
or
PEN AND SWORD BOOKS
1950 Lawrence Rd, Havertown, PA 19083, USA
E-mail: uspen-and-sword@casematepublishers.com
Website: www.penandswordbooks.com

This book is dedicated to all the brave men, women and children who tragically lost their lives at the hands of Japanese military forces during a most brutal period in history.

Contents

Acknowledgements

Writing a book is often a lonely and self-centred business; however, as most writers will tell you, there are always a few people in the background who have offered you advice and support.

Firstly, I must thank my long-suffering wife Liz for putting up with my addiction to the war in the Far East and the long hours I have 'gone missing' while I worked on the manuscript.

To Andrew Snow and all at the Death Railway Museum in Kanchanaburi, Thailand, for their help.

Thanks also to all at Pen & Sword for having the faith to accept this book for publication, particularly Henry Wilson, Matt Jones and my editor, Linne Matthews.

List of Images

Japanese prisoners in the dock during the first war crimes trial held in Rangoon, Burma. These men were charged with the murder of 637 civilians in the village of Kalagon, Burma.

General Tomoyuki Yamashita, the most notorious Japanese officer who was convicted of war crimes, in particular for the 'Rape of Manila' and the Alexandra Hospital Massacre. Yamashita was found guilty of failing to prevent the massacres and atrocities and was sentenced to be executed in February 1946.

General Hideki Tōjō at his trial in Tokyo, 1947. He was found guilty and hanged.

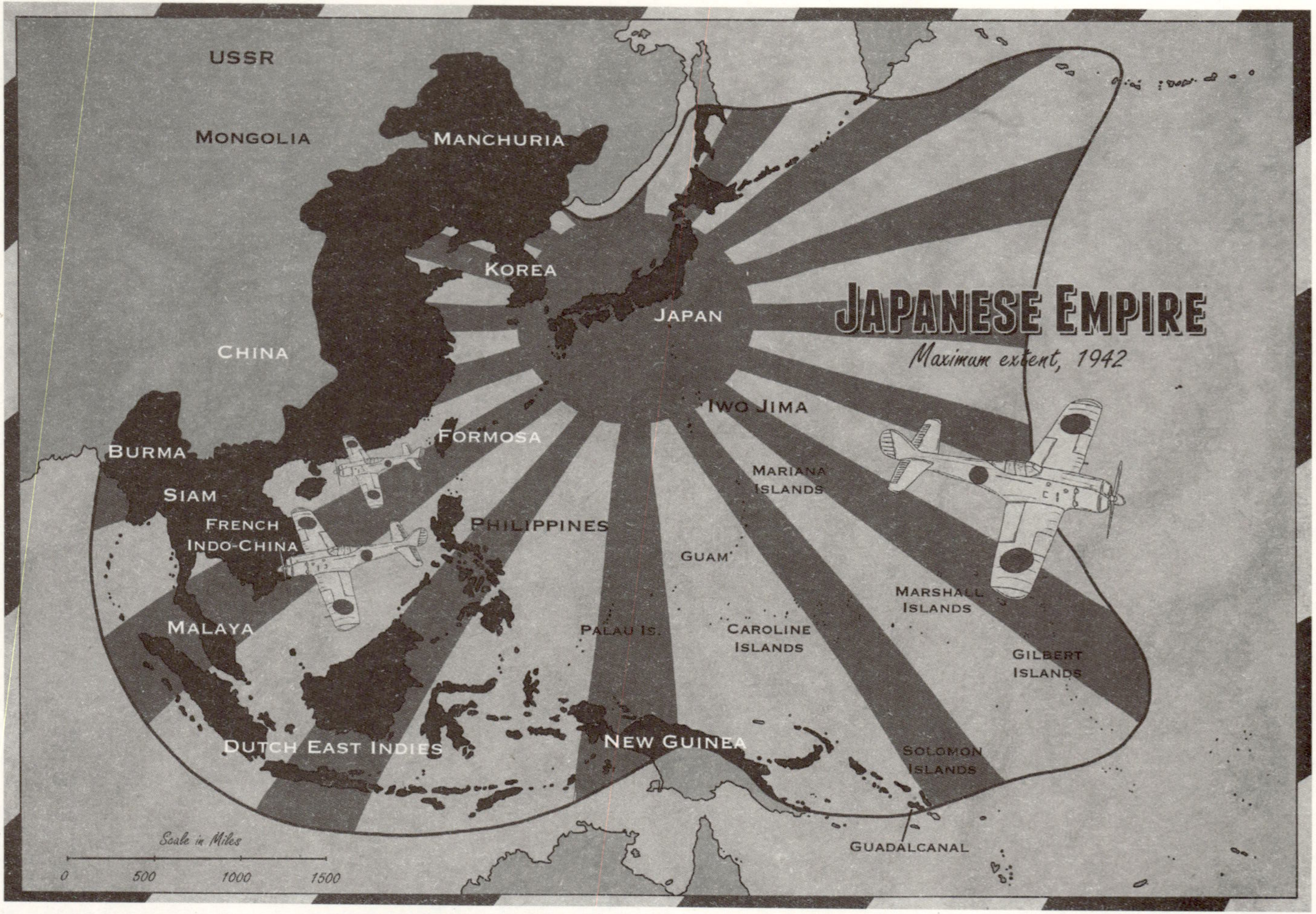

JAPANESE EMPIRE
Maximum extent, 1942
USSR
MONGOLIA
MANCHURIA
KOREA
JAPAN
CHINA
IWO JIMA
FORMOSA
BURMA
SIAM
FRENCH INDO-CHINA
PHILIPPINES
MARIANA ISLANDS
GUAM
MARSHALL ISLANDS
MALAYA
PALAU IS.
CAROLINE ISLANDS
GILBERT ISLANDS
DUTCH EAST INDIES
NEW GUINEA
SOLOMON ISLANDS
GUADALCANAL
Scale in Miles
0
500
1000
1500

Preface

A Japanese soldier

> He would fight without food or water and sustain himself on his ability to withstand pain and hardship that he accepted as part of a soldier's duty. He obeyed orders to commit suicide attacks without question and was happy to know that he would die like a hero for his Emperor. He was ready to be blown to pieces, shot or horribly wounded. Above all he welcomed death.
>
> Ralph Modder, *The Singapore Chinese Massacre*, Horizon Books, 2004

As the title suggests, this book is about atrocities, what they looked like, what they must have felt like to the people carrying them out and for those on the receiving end.

I'm sure some people will ask me what I hope to achieve by bringing such horrors into the public eye. My answer is simple; I have a family link to the war in East Asia, as my father was there. For three and a half years, he was a prisoner of war under a strict and brutal Japanese military machine. The psychological and physical wounds suffered by the victims of Japanese military cruelty have continued to haunt their families (including my own) right up until today.

Whilst many people may shrink at the contents of this book, I would argue that those who do not remember the past are condemned to relive it.

I wish to make it clear that the use of the words in this book that might offend today are in quotations, and were words that were commonly used during the war.

I use the words 'murdered', 'massacred' and 'executed' regularly throughout this book, in the following contexts:

- Murdered, being the unlawful, premeditated killing of one human being by another.

- Massacred, being to deliberately and brutally kill many people in a short period of time.
- Executed, referring to the carrying out a sentence of death on a legally condemned person.

The Japanese used the word 'execution' on numerous occasions during their purges, but the use of the word is misleading, as it gives the impression that the victims of their brutality had a fair trial, resulting in a lawful execution, which in most instances was not the case.

It is also important to consider the use of the word 'democide' in the context of this book, a word that was coined by Rudolph Rummel, an American political scientist and professor at the Indiana University, Yale University, and University of Hawaii. Rummel spent his career studying data on collective violence and war with a view towards helping their resolution or elimination to describe:

> The intentional killing of an unarmed or disarmed person by government agents acting in their authoritative capacity and pursuant to government policy or high command. It covers a wide range of deaths, including forced labour and concentration camp victims, killings by mercenaries and unofficial private groups, extrajudicial summary killings, and mass deaths due to governmental acts of criminal omission and neglect.

Rummel estimated that:

> From the invasion of China in 1937 to the end of World War II, the Japanese military regime murdered near 3,000,000 to over 10,000,000 people, most probably almost 6,000,000 Chinese, Indonesians, Koreans, Filipinos, and Indochinese, among others, including Western prisoners of war. This democide was due to a morally bankrupt political and military strategy, military expediency and custom, and national culture.

During the early part of the twentieth century, it is estimated that around 5 per cent of the casualties in wars were civilian non-combatants, but as the century drew to a close, this figure had risen to around 90 per cent – a quite staggering and sobering statistic.

For many centuries, conquering armies treated prisoners of war with contempt, incarcerating them shackled in dreadful conditions and denying them food and water. It was not until 1785 that an attempt was made to force countries to treat them humanely, when the 'Treaty of Friendship' between Russia and the USA was signed. It was the first global attempt to forbid the keeping of prisoners of war shackled and to treat them humanely.

It was to be another seventy-nine years before attempts were made to formally standardise the treatment of prisoners of war, when the first Geneva Convention was held on 22 August 1864. It was agreed at that convention that wounded and sick soldiers who are out of the battle should be humanely treated, should not be killed, injured, tortured, or subjected to biological experimentation. It included the obligation to respect medical units and establishments, personnel entrusted with the care of the wounded, buildings and material, and medical transports. It also said that wounded and sick soldiers should be collected, cared for, and protected, though they may also become prisoners of war. It was ratified within three years by all the major European powers as well as by many other states.

Forty-three years later, in 1907, the Hague Convention was drawn up – a convention that dwelt on the agreement about what types of weapons, particularly chemical and biological, should be used in war. It stated:

> Prisoners of war must be treated humanely, and their personal property respected. That all captured troops including non-combatants were entitled to prisoner of war status. Work should neither be excessive nor connected with the war. That they must be decently housed and fed as well as their captors. That a proper record of their particulars should be taken and disclosed to those entitled to ask for them, and that the relief provided for them by organisations such as the Red Cross must be given to them.

This was followed twenty-two years later by the second Geneva Convention, forty-seven countries signing it on 27 July 1929, including Japan.

Britain and the USA made it clear to Japan, when war broke out between them in December 1941, that they would observe the Geneva Convention, and asked them to do the same. Japan agreed that they would conform to the Convention and treat all Allied prisoners of war under its statutes, whilst still not formally ratifying it. They were, however, still bound by the

1907 Hague Convention, which they had signed and ratified. Every single one of the pledges they signed was broken time after time, as this book will clearly demonstrate.

Whilst Japanese official policy was to adhere to the Geneva Convention, its officers often lacked the capacity to carry it out.

Most people will agree that wars should be conducted in such a way that non-combatants are protected, and that military discipline is such that casualties are kept to a minimum. The Japanese rode roughshod over this agreement, as you will discover later in this book.

The Japanese original concept was of a South-East Asia Co-prosperity Sphere that would liberate Asian countries from their European colonial rule. This new sphere would, according to their imperial propaganda: 'Establish a new international order seeking co-prosperity for Asian countries and free them from Western colonialism and domination.'

Japanese nationalists, however, saw it as a way to gain resources that were scarce in their homelands. They coveted resource-rich Western colonies such as British Malaya, Burma, American Philippines, French Indo China and the Dutch East Indies. In reality, it was a front to control completely the countries they were to annex, in which puppet governments manipulated local populations and economies for the benefit of Imperial Japan.

During their attempt to create this Greater South-East Asia Co-prosperity Sphere during the 1930s and early 1940s, the Japanese were guilty of carrying out numerous atrocities across the countries they invaded. Many thousands of innocent men, women and children perished at the hands of a brutal military machine.

For three and a half years, my father was a slave labourer on the infamous Thai–Burma Railway, where, along with many of his colleagues, he was tortured and abused on a daily basis. They were robbed of their possessions as well as their dignity, working night and day in atrocious conditions on a project that was very much war related, despite the Hague Convention, which stated that 'work should neither be excessive nor connected with the war'.

Allied prisoners of war in Japanese hands were housed in filthy conditions, with many starved to death and others reduced to walking skeletons. One out of every four of these men were to die of starvation or ill treatment during their captivity.

It was not until the dropping of the atomic bombs on Hiroshima and Nagasaki in early August 1945 that, at 28 years of age, my father realised that he might see his family again and have a life to look forward to. He was one of the lucky ones to survive. My very existence depended on the dropping of those two bombs in August 1945 – there by the grace of God. Along with thousands of other prisoners of war, towards the middle of 1945 my father had been sentenced to death by the Japanese should the Allies ever invade the Japanese homelands. This edict was sent out in an order issued by the Japanese High Command to all prisoner of war camp commanders. A copy of this actual order was found in the safe in one of the camps in Formosa after the war and is now in a US archive. (See Conclusion for exact wording of the document.)

Over seventy-eight years have passed since the war ended in 1945, yet the Japanese government has never acknowledged the atrocities carried out by their military forces, nor has it made an official apology. A handful of extreme right-wing forces in Japan have altered history course books, seeking to depict the war as the liberation of backward nations, and have attempted to reinterpret their atrocities as 'a self-defensive holy war'. Memories of the Asia–Pacific War have faded into the past for many people, but even in Japan today, there is still a sense of disbelief that prevails over the atrocities outlined in this book.

By early March 1942, the Japanese had interned over 140,000 Allied prisoners of war in camps scattered all over the Far East. Around one in four of them were to die of disease, starvation or massacre, before the war ended in August 1945. Over 130,000 civilians were also interned – mainly colonial officials and their families, employees of European companies and the families of Allied servicemen. Once again, one in four were to die of disease, starvation or massacre.

Military historians have estimated that the number of deaths perpetrated or condoned by the Japanese military through massacre, human experimentation, starvation and forced labour during those fourteen years, ranges from 3 to 14 million.

Where possible in this book, I have consulted primary sources of information, but I acknowledge that some of the facts and figures may not be totally accurate, as many are based on the memories of people from both sides who 'were there'. And as we all know, memories can play tricks on people as they grow older. I have done my utmost, however, to verify the statistics, but with events that took place almost eighty years ago, there will always be errors, and I apologise in advance for any I may make. It is well known that over the centuries, history has been recorded from tiny little scraps of information that have been rescued from the ashes; the rest, of course, is often speculation.

Eminent historian Norman Stone said that during the war, the Japanese were: 'A talented people led by maniacs who knew perfectly well that the war would end in disaster but who were determined to keep their honour intact to the final gruesome suicidal point.'

As an author, I will not shy away from the suffering caused by the Japanese military to innocent people, prior to and during the Second World War. The unsavoury facts, no matter how horrific they appear to be, must be put into the public domain.

Japanese atrocities committed in Asia and the Pacific between 1931 and 1945 were of little concern for most of the British people during the decades following the war as they tried to rebuild their lives. The notable exceptions, however, were former prisoners of war like my father, who took his experiences with him to his grave in 1991. His story, and those of his colleagues, have already been well documented in my previous books:

No Mercy from the Japanese:
A Survivor's Account of the Burma Railway and the Hellships 1942–1945

Last Post over the River Kwai:
The 2nd East Surreys in the Far East 1938–1945

Frank Pantridge MC*:*
Japanese Prisoner of War and Inventor of the Portable Defibrillator

Introduction

In an attempt to understand why the Japanese military carried out numerous atrocities during and leading up to the Second World War, it is necessary to look back several centuries and examine a Japanese culture that had been shaped by a system more than a thousand years old. This culture was based on a strict hierarchy and a dependence on martial competition that had its roots in the nation's feudal history.

Up until the sixteenth century, when two Portuguese traders, António da Mota and Francisco Zeimoto, and possibly a third named António Peixoto, landed on the island of Tanegashima in 1543, the Japanese islands had been isolated from the rest of the world for many generations, an isolation that resulted in an extreme racial and cultural xenophobia.

From the early seventeenth century until the 1868 Meiji Restoration, a hereditary military dictatorship known as the Tokugawa shogunate ruled Japan. The warlords of the Japanese islands recruited personal armies to ensure that neighbouring barons did not annex their lands and wealth. They indoctrinated their soldiers into the 'samurai warrior class', a doctrine known as 'bushido' or the 'way of the warrior', promoting honour, obedience, duty and self-sacrifice. Whilst Western methods of technology crept into Japan during the nineteenth and twentieth centuries, its citizens kept true to their traditional values.

During this time, the curriculum in Japanese schools followed a strict military regime. In 1890, an 'Imperial Rescript on Education Code of Ethics' for all children and teachers was introduced, a rescript that contributed to the rise in militarism during the 1930s and 1940s. It reinforced military principles to children at a very early age, with unquestioning loyalty and obedience to the emperor being the main message. Parts of it were read aloud to pupils every morning before lessons commenced.

Patriotism to the emperor was stressed on a daily basis in all subjects including mathematics, where the pupils did calculations about military matters, and in science classes, where searchlights, wireless communications, land mines, torpedoes and explosives were studied.

By 1925, every school in Japan had a military officer on the staff and military training became a key part of the curriculum. Training centres were set up for young Japanese boys, who were required to undertake 400 hours of military instruction every year. Shops specialised in military toys such as guns, helmets, tanks and uniforms, whilst simulated wars were carried out by children in the streets all over the country.

In his book *The Phoenix Cup*, published in 1947, John Morris, a British journalist who lived in Japan prior to the Second World War, writes: 'I had lived in Japan before the Second World War and had seen first-hand the effect which the subtle poison of award education system was humming on the minds of the younger Japanese generation.'

At a Japanese school during the Sino–Japanese War in 1938, a student recalled the mood in his classroom at the time: 'After the war started my friends would talk of nothing else but the brave Japanese and the cowardly Chinks.' He said that the teachers in his school brainwashed them like dogs, urging them to repeat 'Brave Japanese, cowardly Chinks' on a regular basis. These songs whipped up hostility towards China and of course, the term 'Chink' showed a racist contempt.

When a small boy was asked to dissect a frog at a Japanese school in the early 1930s, he burst into tears, his teacher then slapping him around the head and shouting: 'Why are you crying about a lousy frog? When you grow up, you'll have to kill hundreds of Chinks.'

Japanese schoolteachers treated their young pupils with brutality, often beating their small charges around the head with bamboo sticks. They would make them stand in the snow for hours or hold heavy books above their heads until they collapsed from exhaustion. The whole curriculum was based on obedience, the worship of the emperor and militarism.

A veteran of the Pacific War called Yoshio Shinozuka talked about his education in Japan:

> From birth, from primary school, we were taught that the emperor was God and we were his children. We couldn't even enter the school without bowing to the picture of the emperor. Whenever the national anthem was sung, we had to stand to attention. Whenever we saw the rising sun flag we had to bow. Everything was done under the command of God.

After leaving school, many Japanese teenage boys opted to join the military, where their indoctrination into a mindset that 'dying for the emperor was a great honour' continued. During military training, recruits were forced to obtain top results in a strive for perfection, and to achieve any less was seen as failure. Some trainee soldiers even tried to commit suicide if they failed to achieve the highest grades. They were also conditioned to accept that brutality was the response to any setback that they might encounter, and that any enemy of Japan was 'subhuman'.

Young cadets were brainwashed into accepting that they were a super race and graduated with such a thought firmly planted in their minds. They were often humiliated during their military training and subjected to brutal treatment. Author Toshio Iritani wrote that officers justified their cruel behaviour towards their troops by saying: 'I do not beat you because I hate you, I beat you because I care for you; do you think I perform these acts with hands swollen and bloody in the state of madness?'

Such brainwashing and indoctrination resulted in Japanese soldiers being prepared to commit suicide or carry out suicide attacks without question, and to die for their emperor. They were constantly told that if they were captured by the enemy, they would be executed, or if they escaped, they would be executed by their officers when they came back to their regiment, so better to die in combat. This ideology was known as '*gyokusai*'.

In 1908, the Japanese Criminal Code contained the following provisions:

> A commander who allows his unit to surrender to the enemy without fighting to the last man or who concedes a strategic area to the enemy shall be punishable by death. If a commander is leading troops in combat and they are captured by the enemy, even if the commander has performed his duty to the utmost, he shall be punishable by up to six months in prison.

According to Saburō Ienaga, in his book *The Pacific War*, Japan during the 1930s was: 'A Kafkaesque State dictated to the abuse of human rights. On the one hand, the people voluntarily surrendered their rights either because of a largely agrarian, premodern consciousness or because of a conformist, statist education.'

Chapter 1

Unit 731

1931–1944

Morioka – Japan. A cheerful old farmer jokes as he serves rice cakes made by his wife, before switching easily to explaining what it was like to cut open a 30-year-old man who is tied naked to a bed and dissect him alive without anaesthetic. This 72-year-old farmer had been a medical assistant in a Japanese Army medical unit in China in 1933.

> The fellow knew that it was over for him, so he didn't struggle when they led him into the room and tied him down. But when I picked up the scalpel, that's when he began screaming. I cut him open from the chest to the stomach and he screamed terribly, and his face was all twisted in agony. He made this unimaginable sound; he was screaming so horribly. But then finally he stopped. This was all in a day's work for the surgeons, but it really left an impression on me because it was my first time. The prisoner, who was Chinese, was deliberately infected with the plague, as part of a research project to develop plague bombs for use in World War II. After infecting him, we decided to cut him open to see what the disease does to a man's inside.

Asked why he had not anesthetised the prisoner before dissecting him, the farmer explained: 'Vivisection should be done under normal circumstances. If we'd used anaesthesia, that might have affected the body organs and blood vessels that we were examining. So we couldn't have used an anaesthetic.'

When the topic of children came up, the farmer offered another justification: 'Of course, there were experiments on children. But probably their fathers were spies.' (Interview by Nicholas D. Kristof, the *New York Times*, 17 March 1995.)

On 18 September 1931, the Japanese invaded Chinese Manchuria, establishing the puppet state of Manchukuo. A year later, they set up a tropical diseases research facility called Epidemic Prevention and Water Purification Department in the city of Harbin, capital of the Heilongjiang province.

Located in an old sake distillery in an industrial area of the city, the EPWPD was set up to research the production of vaccines for the Japanese armed forces. The man put in charge of the unit was 40-year-old Lieutenant General Shirō Ishii, a Japanese microbiologist. An imperial prince and cousin of Emperor Hirohito, Ishii had achieved a meteoric rise in the Japanese Army, gaining promotion to lieutenant general, the highest rank achievable in the Medical Corps. He enjoyed the support and friendship of key figures within the Japanese High Command, leaving him complete freedom to conduct his research.

Located in a heavily populated area, the EPWPD was soon beset with problems. Ishii became very worried that the nature of the experiments they were carrying out on prisoners might be leaking out into the wider world. In early 1932, he decided to close the unit and within a few months, the complex had been demolished. He was then granted permission to build a new facility in the small village of Beiyinhe, approximately 70 miles south-east of the previous site, by an Imperial Seal of Emperor Hirohito himself.

It was late 1932 when a group of Japanese troops descended without warning on the village. They ordered the inhabitants to load up their belongings and move out within three days, under the threat of death if the order was not obeyed. The troops then proceeded to burn down more than 300 homes and shops within an area of 500 square metres, leaving just one large block that contained the market hall. The residents of Beiyinhe had no idea why they were being evicted, but the sinister reasons for the total elimination of this little village will be explained later.

With the village flattened, the Japanese, using local Chinese labour, immediately began to build a new facility, to be known as Unit 731 or the 'Lumber Mill'. It was made up of around 150 buildings, including two top-secret prisons and three crematoria, all very unusual buildings for a mill. The buildings were surrounded by a 10-foot-high wall topped with barbed wire and electrical fencing, and an airport was built on a neighbouring field to bring in supplies. Japanese guards were posted around the facility and the local people were threatened with arrest if they came near.

When the new facility was opened, Ishii made the following speech to the staff:

> Our God-given mission as doctors is to challenge all varieties of disease-causing microorganisms; to block all roads of intrusion into the human body; to annihilate all foreign matter resident in our bodies; and to devise the most expeditious treatment possible. However, the research work upon which we are now about to embark is the complete opposite of these principles and may cause us some anguish as doctors. Nevertheless, I beseech you to pursue this research, based on the dual thrill of (1) a scientist to exert efforts to probing for the truth in natural science and research into, and discovery of, the unknown world and (2) as a military person, to successfully build a powerful military weapon against the enemy.

Inside the 'Lumber Mill', Ishii proceeded to ignore the vaccine research programme and instigate instead research into biological and chemical weapons. It was now a top-secret prison, a hospital, a medical laboratory, and a chemical research laboratory.

In late 1933, around 600 Chinese political prisoners and guerrillas, detained for anti-Japanese resistance activity, were imprisoned in the mill, where they were fed a nutritious diet. Ishii preferred men under 40 years of age for his research to ensure that he had the best physical specimens on which to test the poisons and germs they were developing. Unit 731's horrific range of experiments was now well under way.

Prisoners in the unit were injected with glanders, typhoid, smallpox, anthrax and dysentery viruses to study how the human body reacted to them. A culture produced from mice with bubonic plague was injected into them, usually resulting in an agonising death. Others had blood slowly taken from them to study how long a person could survive. Prisoners were often dissected without anaesthetic as Ishii was convinced that anaesthesia affected the results of surgery.

Experiments on live prisoners were filmed and sent back to Tokyo, where they were viewed by senior Japanese officers and officials, including Tōjō Hideki, the Japanese prime minister. Prince Mikasa, Hirohito's younger brother, wrote in his memoirs that he was also shown films of Chinese prisoners being marched out onto the Manchurian plain as guinea pigs (*morumotto* in Japanese) for gross experimentation on live subjects.

Whilst most of the prisoners who suffered at the hands of the Japanese in Beiyinhe were killed during its first two years, in late 1934, one group managed to escape. A captive called Li, along with thirty others, overpowered a guard and stole his keys. They were able to unlock their leg irons and make a run for it towards the outer walls, where they were fortunate to find that a rainstorm had knocked out the camp's security system, along with the electrified fencing and searchlights. On reaching the walls, they organised a human chain to climb over them, but when the guards were alerted, Li and ten others were gunned down. The other twenty men managed to climb over the wall, but eight of them were shot as they tried to run away. The other twelve escaped and vanished back into the local Chinese community, where they told the horrific story of what was happening inside the unit.

Ishii continued his gruesome experiments inside Unit 731. Prisoners were forced to have sexual intercourse with others who were known to be infected with syphilis, with the healthier of the two then closely observed to ascertain how the virus was passed on. Female prisoners of childbearing age were also forcibly impregnated, with live dissections often taking place to find out how their organs reacted to syphilis. One anonymous member of Ishii's staff told an interviewer after the war:

> At first, we infected women with syphilis by injection. But this method did not produce real research results. Syphilis is normally transmitted through direct contact. Investigating the course of this disease can offer no useful results unless it is acquired this way. And so, we followed a system of direct infection through sexual contact.

It wasn't just Chinese political prisoners who were subject to horrific experiments; homeless beggars would be picked up off the streets as cannon fodder. These unfortunate victims were now called 'logs' (*maruta* in Japanese). One Unit 731 technician called Yoshio Shinozuka, who carried out several vivisections on live subjects, recalled conversations amongst the staff: 'How many logs did you down today? At my place we downed two.' Shinozuka wrote about his gruesome experiments in 1997:

> I still remember clearly the first vivisection I participated in. I knew the Chinese individual we dissected because I had taken his blood once for testing. At the vivisection I could not meet his eyes because of the hate he had in his glare at me. This intelligent looking man was

> systematically infected with plague germs. As the disease took its toll, his face and body became totally black. Still alive, he was brought on a stretcher by the special security forces to the autopsy room. Transferred to the autopsy table, the chief pathologist ordered us to wash his body. I used a rubber hose and a deck brush to wash him since this was my first vivisection, I think I was somewhat sloppy in washing him. I remember feeling somewhat hesitant and using the brush on his face. Watching me, the chief pathologist, with scalpel in hand, impatiently signalled me to hurry up. I closed my eyes and forced myself to scrub the man's face with the deck brush. The chief pathologists listened to the man's heartbeat with a stethoscope and then the procedure started. The man's organs were methodically excised one by one, and I did as I was ordered to. I put them in a culturing can we had already prepared.

In other experiments, prisoners were deprived of food and water to find out how long it took them to die. Others were locked into low-pressure chambers until their eyes popped from their sockets to find out how low a pressure the human body could take. Prisoners were injected with horse blood to see if it could be a substitute for human blood. They were hung upside down to see how long it took for them to choke to death. They were crushed with heavy objects. They were electrocuted. They were placed into centrifuges and spun until they died. They were exposed to lethal doses of X-rays and injected with different blood types. These were some of the most horrific experiments ever carried out on human beings.

A former army major and technician in Unit 731 gave the following testimony anonymously after the war. (At the time of the interview, he was an emeritus professor at a Japanese national university.)

> In 1943, I attended a poison gas test held at the Unit 731 test facilities. A glass-walled chamber about three metres square and two metres high was used. Inside of it, a Chinese man was blindfolded, with his hands tied around a post behind him. The gas was adamsite* and as the gas filled the chamber the man went into violent coughing convulsions and began to suffer excruciating pain. More than ten doctors and technicians

* Adamsite is an odourless crystalline organic compound employed in vaporous form as a lung irritant. It appears as a yellow smoke that irritates eyes, lungs, and mucous membranes and causes sneezing, vomiting, and acute discomfort in the nose, throat, and chest.

> were present. After I had watched for about ten minutes, I could not stand it anymore, and left the area. I understand that other types of gasses were also tested there.

Probably the most sadistic experiment allegedly carried out at Unit 731, one that could not have any conceivable military application, was where they tested the time it took for three-day-old babies to freeze to death. A member of the unit, who gave an interview in the 1980s, said that he had used twenty children in experiments where they were exposed to sub-zero temperatures to establish their resistance index to frostbite.

Pregnant test subjects were also infected with various diseases, exposed to chemical weapons, crash injuries, bullet wounds and shrapnel injuries to study their effects on the foetuses. Babies that were born in the unit were also used in medical experiments, their corpses simply burned afterwards. Doctors even experimented on a three-day-old baby, measuring the temperature with a needle stuck inside the infant's middle finger. Usually a hand of a three-day-old infant is clenched into a fist, but by sticking the needle in, the middle finger could be kept straight to make the experiment easier. Older children were also used in experiments and no child prisoner ever survived.

Experiments into the effects of mustard gas was tested on prisoners. They were put into trenches and bombarded with the gas to see how they reacted, whilst others were locked in sealed rooms and phosphine gas pumped in. Within twenty-four hours, they became critically ill with respiratory tract irritation and pneumonia. In another test, subjects were injected with 15 milligrams of potassium cyanide, again monitored until they lost consciousness and died.

Experiments were carried out into the effects of high-voltage electric shocks on humans. Endo Sabura, an officer in the unit at the time, wrote in his diary about electric shocks on patients: '20,000 volts – several jolts of that voltage, not enough to kill the subject, 45,000 volts severe jolts not enough, after several minutes of continuous currents the subject was burnt to death.'

Yoshimura Hisato, a physiologist in Unit 731 who had a special interest in hypothermia, used human subjects to test their reactions to frostbite. He submerged their limbs in a tub of water filled with ice, held them there until the limbs were frozen solid and timed how long it took for the human body to develop frostbite. According to one of the witnesses to his experiments, 'their limbs made a sound like a plank of wood when struck with a cane'. Once frostbite had set in, Hisato then tried different methods for thawing the frozen appendage, such as plunging the limbs into hot water, over an open fire, or leaving the subject untreated overnight. He was then able to prove scientifically that the best treatment for frostbite was to immerse the appendage in water around 100 degrees, but never more than 122 degrees.

In other experiments, human subjects were locked up and deprived of food and water until they died, to find out how long humans could survive without sustenance. Heavy objects were dropped on prisoners staked to the ground to discover the effects of crash injuries. In another gruesome experiment, a prisoner had his hands cut off and sewn back on the opposite way round.

As high G-forces on pilots and falling paratroopers were of concern to the Japanese military, the medical teams studied this by loading prisoners into a large centrifuge. They were then spun at higher and higher speeds until they lost consciousness or died, which usually happened between 10 and 15 G.

Another area of special interest to the researchers was the human brain. Prisoners would have their heads broken open, usually with an axe, the brain removed from the skull and experiments carried out on it. The body would also be dissected while still warm and then cremated. Other experiments involved hanging prisoners upside down by their feet to ascertain how long it would take them to die.

A medical worker based in Unit 731 called Takeo Wane said that he once saw a large glass jar in which a Western man was pickled in formaldehyde. The life expectancy of prisoners at the unit was usually no more than thirty days.

One medical assistant recalled:

> A prisoner was taken from his cell into the dissecting room. He was stripped and placed on the table screaming, trying to fight back. He was strapped down, still screaming frightfully. One of the doctors stuffed a towel into his mouth, then with one quick slice of the scalpel he was opened up. He did not die immediately after being cut open as the doctors examined his heart, liver, intestines, and other organs. Eventually he died from the steady loss of blood and body tissues.

During the early 1940s, groups of boys, some as young as 13, were sent from Japan to Unit 731, where they were given a medical education, and in some cases these boys dissected living human beings.

With the Japanese war in China continuing, Ishii and his staff were also carrying out experiments on chemical and biological weapons. Prisoners were given drinks, including tea, coffee and in some cases beer, that had been mixed with an organism to study its effects on the human body, including *Salmonella enterica* Typhi, a Gram-negative bacterium that is responsible for typhoid fever.

Anthrax-loaded sweets were given out to the children around Harbin, and many Chinese cities and towns were sprayed from Japanese aircraft with plague-infected fleas.

By 1940, with their war with China raging, the Japanese dropped German-made bombs on hundreds of heavily populated communities, whilst on the ground, their troops dropped cholera and typhoid cultures into wells and ponds. The purpose of this bacteriological warfare was to spread epidemic diseases on a large scale in areas still under Chinese control and cause mass extermination. Tens of thousands of Chinese people died of bubonic plague, cholera, anthrax and other diseases due to such methods.

It has been estimated that between 10,000 and 12,000 men, women and children were murdered during experiments at Unit 731 and other Japanese so-called medical establishments, and that as many as 250,000 more were killed in field tests.

By early August 1945, with the Japanese surrender looming, Unit 731 was closed down and the buildings demolished. However, as they were constructed to a high standard, they were difficult to destroy, with several blocks remaining intact.

In a last-ditch effort to cause mayhem, plague-infected rats and fleas were released into the surrounding villages, resulting in the deaths of thousands of innocent Chinese civilians.

When the war was drawing to close in early August 1945, Ishii, along with his senior colleagues, escaped back to Japan, taking with them most of the documents and films of the bizarre experiments carried out in the unit. Most of the junior staff who were left behind were captured by the Russians as they tried to escape, and were simply slaughtered, whilst the remaining doctors were taken to secret police headquarters in Khabarovsk. There they were tortured before being worked to death in Stalin's camps in north-east Siberia.

After the war, Stalin requested that Ishii be arrested and brought to trial in Moscow for war crimes, but the evil doctor decided to go into hiding in

Japan. He planted a story in a Japanese newspaper that he had been killed, his friends even going to the extent of staging his funeral, but his freedom was not to last as he was located and arrested by American intelligence authorities in January 1946.

Despite Stalin's request, General Douglas MacArthur exonerated Ishii and his senior doctors of war crimes in exchange for handing over all his documents relating to the results of his experiments, one of which extended to 12,000 pages.

It is said by some historians that in 1951, Ishii was secretly flown by MacArthur to the United States, where he lectured at Fort Detrick about Unit 731's human experiments, but others said that after the war his exact whereabouts or occupation were unknown from 1947. Richard Drayton, a Cambridge University history lecturer, claimed that Ishii later went to Maryland to advise on bioweapons. Another source says he stayed in Japan, where he opened a clinic, performing examinations and treatments for free. What is clear, though, is that Ishii died in Tokyo on 9 October 1959 and is buried in a cemetery on the outskirts of the city.

After the war, many of the other senior doctors from Unit 731 were promoted to senior posts in medicine, industry and in universities in Japan. In 1951, three of the most senior doctors from that unit set up Japan's first blood bank service using the expertise that they had built up. Some of them dominated the Ministry of Health and the board of the Japan Medical Society. Other staff members such as Naito Ryoichi and Kitano Masaji went on to form important pharmaceutical companies.

On 29 August 1982, Ishii's daughter was interviewed by the *Japan Times* about her father's experiments. She told the journalist:

> What my father did or was alleged to have done in the line of duty as a medical officer and soldier in the Imperial Japanese Army, shall be denounced by any moral standard. Even so, one must not forget that it all happened under extremely abnormal circumstances. It was war.

During the war years, the Japanese set up other biological and chemical warfare units in areas of China and in Japan itself. In Changchun, the largest city of Jilin province in China, they set up Unit 100, a facility that specialised in plant and animal biological warfare. In Beijing, they set up Unit 1855, which specialised in cholera epidemics. In Guangzhou (Canton), they set up Unit 8604, and in Inner Mongolia, they set up Unit 2646, also known as Unit 80, which was engaged in secret human experiments.

A Japanese doctor called Ken Yuasa confirmed in Tokyo many years after the war that human experimentation was commonplace in China during the war years. When he was posted to Shanxi province in north-central China in 1942, he was required to perform an experiment on two Chinese men, and said:

> The men were brought in, stripped naked and given a general anesthetic. Then I, along with two others, began practising various kinds of surgery: first an appendectomy, then an amputation of an arm and finally a tracheotomy. After we had finished, we killed the patient.

Yuasa also said that he had cultivated typhoid germs in test tubes and sent them to army units and that he was deeply apologetic for the acts he had carried out.

Right up until the end of the twentieth century, victims of Japan's biological warfare in China were still suffering from its effects; many of them had lived for years with painful festering ulcers on their legs, which never healed. (An affliction that was called rotten leg syndrome.) In 2002, a group of Chinese survivors of Japanese experiments, along with relatives of victims who had died, filed a lawsuit against the Japanese government, but it proved unsuccessful.

Many historians allege that that Emperor Hirohito was aware of the human experiments going on in Unit 731 but did nothing to stop them. On 13 August 1985, Britain's Independent Television broadcast a documentary entitled *Unit 731 – Did the Emperor Know?* In an interview with Lieutenant Colonel Murray Sanders, the first US investigator into Unit 731 after the war ended, he claimed that Hirohito knew about Ishii's work. He also claimed that General Douglas MacArthur authorised him to make a deal with the Japanese if they co-operated with United States biological warfare scientists – quite strong evidence that a deal was done behind closed doors.

For many years, the names of the members of Unit 731 were kept secret, until as late as 2018, when *The Guardian*'s Tokyo correspondent was given the names of 3,607 people by the country's National Archives. This was in a request by Katsuo Nishiyama, a professor at Shiga University of Medical

Science, in a move that reignited the public debate over Japanese atrocities committed in occupied China before and during the Second World War.

Nishiyama told *The Mainichi* newspaper:

> This is the first time that an official document showing the real names of almost all members of Unit 731 has been disclosed. The list is important evidence that supports testimony by those involved. Its discovery will be a major step toward unveiling concealed facts.

The document lists members of the Kwantung Army's Epidemic Prevention and Water Purification Department – the unit's official name – and is dated 1 January 1945. It includes the names, ranks and contact details of more than 1,000 army medics, as well as dozens of doctors, surgeons, nurses and engineers.

Other than the above, researchers found no new classified evidence related to General Ishii's experiments or the unit's treatment of prisoners. A few documents became available as the years passed, adding more evidence to the already well-documented facts about Japanese abuse of prisoners in Unit 731. As for the question of Unit 731's alleged experimentation on captured American servicemen, despite exhaustive searches in intelligence, military and diplomatic records, no definitive evidence was found.

The were, however, several documents that turned up in the US in 1960. Three important documents, translated from Japanese to English and each more than 100 pages long, detail Unit 731's clinical observations of the day-by-day spread of various pathogens through the bodies of helpless prisoners whom Japanese doctors subjected to experiments. The US government declassified these key documents, titled 'The Report of A' (anthrax), 'The Report of G' (glanders), and 'The Report of Q' (bubonic plague) in 1960. They were made available to the public at the US Library of Congress.

Chapter 2

The Rape of Nanking

December 1937

In 1931, the Japanese Army invaded Chinese Manchuria, setting up the puppet state of Manchukuo and installing the former boy emperor of the Ching Dynasty, Henry Pu, as its leader. Seven years later, in 1937, they had control of large sections of China.

On 7 July that year, an incident occurred at the Marco Polo Bridge near the town of Wanping outside Peking (now Beijing), an incident that many historians claim was the start of the Second World War. The exact details of what happened that day have been clouded in controversy, but it is alleged that Japanese troops training near the bridge were shot at by Chinese troops who were patrolling nearby. A Japanese soldier was unaccounted for after the incident, and when his officers asked the Chinese if they could search for him in Wanping, the request was refused. Regardless, the Japanese forced their way into the town, sparking a military conflict that started the Sino–Japanese War.

A month later, on 13 August, the Japanese attacked the Chinese city of Shanghai. The taking of the city proved much more difficult than the Japanese high command had anticipated, as Chiang Kai-shek, the nationalist leader, had employed his best troops to defend it. Several hundred Japanese soldiers were killed before the city eventually fell on 26 November, after more than three months of fighting. Japanese troops went on the rampage, looting, raping, and murdering surrendered Chinese troops along with innocent Chinese civilians. (See Chapter 14, Other Atrocities.).

With Shanghai now under their control, the Japanese then poured eastwards towards the Chinese capital of Nanking, plundering, and murdering everyone in their path. Small towns and villages were bombed and set on fire; in some cases, whole cities were razed to the ground.

Japanese troops poured into the ancient city of Suchow (now called Suzhou) near Tai Hu Lake, just to the west of Nanking, in early November, and by the beginning of December they reached Nanking. The poorly equipped and trained Chinese defenders were no match for the invaders, and after only twelve days of fighting, the city fell, leaving more than half a million civilians and 90,000 troops trapped.

Japanese troops then went on the rampage like hordes of wild animals, wreaking havoc among the local population. One eyewitness described the scenes: 'Everyone in the city appeared to be considered as prey, and the members of the victorious army had set upon the prize to commit unlimited violence.'

Seven thousand Chinese troops who had surrendered on the outskirts of the city were marched to a nearby village, where they were all killed, with other groups transported in trucks to remote locations near the mountains north of Nanking, where they were also annihilated. Footage and still photographs taken by the Japanese in Nanking at that time showed smiling soldiers using Chinese prisoners for bayonet practice before decapitating them. Some were mowed down by machine-gun fire whilst others were tied-up, soaked with gasoline and burned alive. Bodies were displayed on the streets with severed heads put up on poles.

The Japanese soldiers then turned their attention to the women of Nanking, when with no respect for age, they proceeded to sexually abuse and rape them, some as old as 70 and girls as young as 8. Pregnant women were raped, many having their stomachs cut open and their foetuses ripped out after the acts had been carried out. Men were even forced to rape their own daughters, sons forced to rape their mothers, whilst the rest of the family were forced to watch. It has been estimated by historians that more than 20,000 women (with some estimates even higher, at around 80,000) were raped.

The Japanese soldiers raided shops, then killed the shopkeepers by setting the buildings on fire after locking them inside. The Chinese population were stopped at random, and if they were found to have nothing of value in their possession, they were simply killed on the spot. Nanking was running with blood.

After the war, a Japanese soldier who had been in Nanking at the time was asked by an American journalist whether he felt pity for the Chinese who were murdered, and he replied:

> I was a young soldier when our troops occupied Nanking. Our officers told us we could kill and rape as many of 'the Chinese enemy' as we

> pleased. There were some of us however, who did not like the idea, including myself. When we did not join the others in shooting and bayoneting the civilians, we were ridiculed and made fun of. Our troops were holding competitions among themselves to see who could shoot or bayonet to death the most Chinese within a specific time. Eventually, I was persuaded to join them. A sergeant told me with a laugh, 'Killing a Chinese is just like killing a dog! You'll feel nothing! Try it and you'll see!' My first victim was an old Chinese woman. I aimed my rifle at her head. I pressed the trigger. I saw her brains splatter on the brick wall behind her. The other soldiers cheered and encouraged me. After that, I killed many Chinese of all ages, even children. I did not feel any remorse. I also raped young girls before killing them. I became involved in the frenzy of killing and everything else that was going on. Later I felt disgusted and horrified at what my comrades and I did. I now spend my days praying for forgiveness.

As the new year dawned in January 1938, Nanking was littered with putrefying corpses, the Qinhuai River ran red with blood, its bed so saturated with bodies that troops could walk across it.

With so many bodies littering the city, the Japanese began to get concerned about the spread of disease and its effects on their troops, so they began to change their methods of killing. Chinese people were herded into pits, where they were buried alive, whilst others had petrol poured over them and were burned alive. Japanese soldiers were happy to be photographed with their swords raised over their intended victims or posing over the slaughter pits.

By mid-1938, news of the atrocities in Nanking began to appear in Japanese and American newspapers. The *Japan Advertiser* published an account about the decapitation of Chinese people in a contest between two officers that was described as sport. Initially, the stories published in the United States were met with scepticism, as the American public could not believe that such acts were happening.

Japanese journalists who had arrived at Nanking to report on the invasion of the city were horrified by the atrocities their troops were carrying out. One correspondent, called Imai Masatake, reported:

> On Hisiakwan wharves, there was the dark silhouette of a mound of dead bodies. About fifty to one hundred people were toiling there,

> dragging bodies from the mountain of corpses, and throwing them into the Yangtze River. The bodies dripped blood, some of them still alive and moaning weakly, their limbs twitching. The labourers were busy working in total silence, as in a pantomime. In the dark, one could barely see the opposite bank of the river. On the pier was a field of glistening mud under the moon's dim light. Wow! that's all blood!
>
> After a while, the coolies had done their job of dragging the corpses, and the soldiers lined them up along the river. Rat-tat-tat of machine gunfire could be heard. The coolies fell backwards into the river and were swallowed by the raging currents. The pantomime was over. A Japanese officer on this at the scene estimated that 20,000 persons had been executed.

A group of American and European citizens living in Nanking when it fell, mainly doctors, businessmen and missionaries, took it upon themselves to establish a safe international safety zone, declaring a 2½ square mile area of the city as a neutral area, off limits to Japanese troops. This brave group of people risked their lives on quite a few occasions to try to aid the Chinese population.

A German businessman and Nazi member called John Rabe was so appalled and disgusted to see innocent Chinese people being murdered by Japanese soldiers, that he appealed to Adolf Hitler to put pressure on Japan to prevent such atrocities. Hitler simply ignored his appeal. Rabe's diary was published in 1996, highlighting the full extent of what happened in the city. It reads:

> It is not until we tour the city that we learn the extent of destruction. We come across corpses every 100 to 200 yards. The bodies of civilians that I examined had bullet holes in their backs. These people had presumably been fleeing and were shot from behind. The Japanese march through the city in groups of ten to twenty soldiers and loot the shops … I watched with my own eyes as they looted the café of our German baker Herr Kiessling. Hempel's hotel was broken into as well, as almost every shop on Chung Shang and Taiping Road. Two Japanese soldiers have climbed over the garden wall and are about to break into our house. When I appear, they give the excuse that they saw two Chinese soldiers climb over the wall. When I show them my party

> badge, they return the same way. In one of the houses in the narrow street behind my garden wall, a woman was raped, and then wounded in the neck with a bayonet. I managed to get an ambulance so we can take her to Kulou Hospital. … Last night up to 1,000 women and girls are said to have been raped, about 100 girls at Ginling Girls' College alone. You hear nothing but rape. If husbands or brothers intervene, they're shot. What you hear and see on all sides is the brutality and bestiality of the Japanese soldiers. I am totally puzzled by the conduct of the Japanese, on the one hand they want to be recognised and treated as a great power, on a par with European powers, on the other they are currently displaying a crudity brutality and bestiality that bears no comparison except with the hordes of Genghis Khan.

John Rabe gave a series of lectures in Germany after he came back to Berlin on 15 April 1938, during which he said in relation to Nanking: 'We Europeans put the number of civilian casualties at about 50,000 to 60,000.'

Minnie Vautrin, the president of Ginling College in Nanking when the Japanese took over the city, along with Tsen Shui-Fang, a washer assistant and trained nurse, turned the college into a refugee camp for women and children. This camp gave shelter and food to more than 10,000 refugees in a small campus designed for around 3,000. Vautrin writes in her diary:

> Thirty girls were taken from their language school last night, and today I have heard scores of heart-breaking stories of girls who were taken. One of the girls was twelve years old. Food, bedding, and money have been taken from people. I suspect every house in the city has been entered yet again and robbed. A truck passed in which there were eight or ten girls, and as it passed, they called out 'save our lives'. From a military point of view the taking of Nanking may be considered a victory for the Japanese army but judging it from the moral law it is a defeat and a national disgrace which will hinder cooperation and friendship with China for years to come and forever lose the respect of those living in Nanking today. If only the thoughtful people in Japan who could know what is happening in Nanking. …
>
> Oh God control the cruel beastliness of the soldiers in Nanking tonight, comfort the heartbroken mothers and fathers whose innocent sons have been shot today and guard the young women and girls through

the long agonising hours of this night. Speed the day when wars will be no more when the kingdom will come thy will be done on earth as it is in heaven.

Some Japanese soldiers also spoke out after the war about the atrocities carried out in Nanking. A private called Shimada Toshio recalled his baptism of blood:

> A Chinese prisoner had been tied by his hands and ankles to a pole on each side of him. Fifty new recruits were lined up to bayonet him. My emotion must have been paralysed. I felt no mercy on him. He eventually started asking us, 'come on hurry up,' we couldn't stick the right spot. So, he said again 'hurry up' which meant he wanted to die quickly. I found it difficult because my bayonet stuck in him like tofu.
> (British *Daily Mail*, 3 June 2012)

An Italian diplomat based in Manchuria in 1938 wrote at the time: 'The nations of the world are committing a most terrible mistake in dealing with the Japanese as though they were a civilised people. It is a grievous error, and one likely to prove catastrophic in its consequences.'

How right he was proved to be.

One American journalist, who got out of Nanking just before it fell, wrote in the *Chicago Daily News* on 15 December 1937:

> The story of Nanking's fall is a story of indescribable panic and confusion among the entrapped Chinese defenders, followed by a reign of terror by the conquering army that cost thousands of lives, many of them innocent ones, because the Japanese chose the course of systematic extermination. Streets throughout the city were littered with the bodies of civilians and abandoned Chinese equipment and uniforms, and the last thing we saw as we left the city was a band of 300 Chinese being methodically executed before the wall near the waterfront, where already corpses were piled knee deep. Patrols of Japanese soldiers moved through the streets, searched houses, and arrested droves of people as suspected plainclothes soldiers. Few of them ever came back but those who did said their companions had been slaughtered without even a summary trial. I witnessed one of these execution parties and I have

> seen the grim results of others. What is more difficult, I have had to listen to the wailing and sobbing of women pleading for the return of sons and husbands they will never see again.

A Japanese journalist called Tatsuzo wrote an account based on first-hand observation of atrocities committed by Japanese troops in Nanking. He used phrases like 'jabbing it into her three times', 'slashing the head and breasts with a sword' and 'the smell of fresh blood'. These phrases were all deleted from the first published version before the entire article was banned.

Ishikawa later wrote a novel about the Nanking atrocities entitled *Soldiers Alive*. It was immediately banned from publication and not seen by the Japanese public until 1945, when censorship was lifted.

Uno Shintarō, a Japanese soldier in the China campaign, was interviewed after the war for the book *Japan at War: An Oral History*, written by Haruko Taya Cook and her husband. Shintarō told them:

> I personally severed more than forty heads [of Chinese prisoners]. Today, I no longer remember each of them well. It might sound extreme, but I can almost say that if more than two weeks went by without my taking a head, I didn't feel right. Physically, I needed to be refreshed. I would go to the stockade and bring someone out. … I'd [behead them] on the riverbank, by the regimental headquarters. … I sometimes botched the job. The prisoners were physically weakened by torture. … They tended to move. … Sometimes I'd hit the shoulder. Once a lung popped out, almost like a balloon. … Looking at that, I felt ecstasy. But I'm not that way today.

Shiro Azuma, another Japanese soldier who took part in war crimes in China, openly admitted to his deeds after the war when he published his diary in 2006. He said:

> War was about winning or losing. We didn't think about humanity at all. We believed we could do anything to win. When we won the war against China, we were very arrogant. When we went searching for food, we found women hiding, we thought ok they looked tasty, so we raped them. But every single time a woman was raped the soldiers would kill her. I was ordered to kill three farmers suspected of being Chinese

> soldiers, one of them reminded me of my father and so I wasn't all that willing. I kept cutting into his head, into his skull instead of his neck. The blood spurted out. My pal Majima shouted, 'you're too high' and I tried again and chopped his head off, this incident has stayed with me to this day. When I tried to cut off the first one, either the farmer moved or I mis-aimed. I ended up slicing off just part of his skull. Blood spurted upwards. I swung again… and this time I killed him. … We were taught that we were a superior race since we lived only for the sake of a human god—our emperor. But the Chinese were not. So we held nothing but contempt for them. … There were many rapes, and the women were always killed. When they were being raped, the women were human. But once the rape was finished, they became pig's flesh.

He also talks about one of his officers called Mitsuharu Hashimoto, who he alleges murdered a Chinese civilian:

> Hashimoto put a Chinese civilian into a mailbag, soaked it with kerosene, and burned the bag to entertain his comrades. Afterwards, he placed a hand grenade inside the bag and threw it into a river to create a stimulating high.

American journalist Edgar Snow, who was in China at that time, provided the following eyewitness account:

> Thousands of men were led out of the [Nanjing International Safety] Zone, ostensibly for labour battalions, and lined up and machine-gunned. Sometimes groups were used for bayonet exercises. When the victors grew bored with such mild sport they tied their victims, poured kerosene over their heads, and cremated them alive. Others were taken out to empty trenches and told to simulate Chinese soldiers. Japanese officers then led their men in assaults to capture these 'enemy positions' and bayoneted the unarmed defenders.

By November 1939, back in Tokyo, Japanese war minister Itagaki became so concerned about reports of atrocities carried out by troops in China, and their effects on the IJA's good name, that he drew up special orders. These were sent out to all army commanders in China, referring to 'objectionable conduct' by returning soldiers, which was to be stopped. It was not war crimes committed by the soldiers that he was referring to, but to the fact that they were telling friends and relations about them.

Prince Asaka, the son-in-law of Emperor Meiji and uncle by marriage to Emperor Hirohito, was in temporary command of the Japanese forces as they approached Nanking. On 3 December 1937, he issued an order to the troops: 'Kill all captives.' Asaka remained in charge until February 1938, when he was recalled to Japan.

After the war, officials acting under the direction of the Supreme Commander of the Allied Powers (SCAP) interrogated Asaka about his involvement in the Nanking Massacre, but he was never brought before the International Military War Crimes Tribunal for prosecution. Lieutenant General Iwane Matsui succeeded Asaka as commander of Japanese troops in Nanking and at the war crimes tribunals after the war, he was found guilty and hanged in Tokyo. (See page 165)

It has been estimated that more than 12 million people fled from Nanking when the Japanese invaded. The full extent of Japanese war crimes in China will probably never be known, but for the Chinese people they will never be forgotten. Despite photographic and independent eyewitness accounts, the Japanese government has still not acknowledged the full story of the slaughter, rape and looting that took place at Nanking in 1937.

An Italian diplomat, Amleto Vespa, living in Manchuria in 1938, is quoted as saying:

> The nations of the world are committing a most terrible mistake in dealing with the Japanese as though they were a civilised people. It is the grievous error, and one likely to prove catastrophic in its consequences.

Chapter 3

Murder in the Philippines

1941–1945

On 8 December 1941, just hours after they attacked Pearl Harbor, Japanese forces, led by Lieutenant General Masaharu Homma and directed by general Tomoyuki Yamashita, attacked the American administered colony of the Philippines. The American and Filipino defenders under the command of General Douglas MacArthur were totally unprepared for the invasion and were defeated in less than a month. Around 23,000 American troops and 100,000 Filipinos were either killed or captured. Atrocities in the Philippines were about to begin.

With the islands now under their control, the Japanese proceeded to conduct mop-up operations, capturing Filipino soldiers, and executing more than 54,000 civilians including children.

Pregnant Filipino women were brutally murdered, their bellies cut open, and foetuses ripped out, whilst others were shot trying to run away. For the following three and a half years, Japanese soldiers carried out numerous atrocities on the civilian population of the Philippines.

A chilling order was sent out from Tokyo to all its forces:

> The Americans who have penetrated into Manila have about 1,000 troops, and there are several thousand Filipino soldiers under the Commonwealth Army and the organized guerrillas. Even women and children have become guerrillas. All people on the battlefield with the exception of Japanese military personnel, Japanese civilians, and special construction units will be put to death.

This order was obeyed to the letter and a number of executions were carried out on local government officials and former military officers. Chinese Embassy staff were rounded up, massacred, and buried in the Manila Chinese Cemetery.

In June 1942, a young woman was taken by force to a house in Tagbilaran, where a Japanese officer called Colonel Mint ripped off her clothes, tied her hands to the bed and raped her. The following night, the young woman managed to escape to a nearby island by jumping out of the window and was able to tell her story.

Evidence of the treatment of Filipino civilians by the Japanese military was given by a nurse called Nena Alban to the war crimes tribunals:

> The Japanese Army was occupying the grounds of San Beda College. On the first afternoon I saw four Filipinos beheaded by Japanese soldiers. Later I saw two more and thereafter seven more who were made to kneel across a hole in the ground and were beheaded. Again later, I saw ten more beheaded and saw four Filipinos killed by being thrown headfirst on the concrete pavement. I saw Filipinos tortured, boxed, kicked, beaten with heavy wooden sticks. I saw twenty Filipinos tied up and then tortured in many ways. When they screamed or cried, they were placed under the very hot sun. Another group of Filipinos were placed under the sun and hit in the stomach and beaten in many ways and when they were sleeping, water was thrown on them. I saw other groups held in the stock by the legs, in two groups. Their hands were also held in the stock. They were pushed back against the barbed wire fence and were burned with cigarettes, and some were burned by pieces of flaming wood put under their armpits. I saw two more Filipinos beaten to death. I saw nine or more Filipinos bayoneted through the eyes by Japanese soldiers, I saw at least seven Filipinos have their tongues pulled out by pliers.

Japanese soldiers went berserk all across the Philippines, with little or no control by their officers. One on occasion, twenty-four Filipino men and three women were tied with hands behind their backs and then pulled to a thicket, where they were beheaded. A 3-month-old baby was thrown into the air and impaled on a bayonet.

An 11-year-old Filipino girl called Narisa Claveria was seized by the Japanese when they entered her village. Her father, the headmen of the village, was also seized, tied to a tree, and skinned alive, whilst her mother was raped. Three of her siblings tried to defend their parents but they were bayoneted. The family home was burned down and Narisa and another sister were taken away and gang-raped. She told the story later, when she was grown up:

> Whenever the Japanese thought about it, they would just rape us … we women couldn't say no, we couldn't refuse them. We had to go along with it otherwise they'd hurt us. We had a terrible time. We almost couldn't get up from our beds because of the pain. Because it's not just one Japanese, there were loads of them. They would just rape anybody they wanted to.

In March 1944, a young Filipino woman was found by Japanese soldiers hiding in the grass near Canangay, a city on the island of Leyte. An officer grabbed her, took her into a hut, tore off her clothes and proceeded to cut off her breasts with his Samurai sword. He then set the hut on fire and left her to die. Later that same year, a Japanese patrol entered the city of Dapitan on the island of Mindanao and machine-gunned and bayoneted around 500 people in a church. On 1 October 1944, around fifty Japanese soldiers entered a hospital at Barrio Umagos, also on Mindanao. After bayoneting two Filipino guards and one civilian, they proceeded to bayonet patients in their beds before burning the buildings down with the bodies still inside.

American prisoners of war also suffered at the hands of their Japanese captors. Two days before Christmas 1944, fifteen men were taken from their prison cells and driven to a cemetery on the outskirts of San Fernando, Pampanga, where a grave had been dug. They were marched from their trucks to the edge of the grave and forced to kneel, before being bayoneted and decapitated.

A Japanese medical auxiliary called Akira Makino, who took part in atrocities, confessed to cutting open the bodies of ten Filipino prisoners, including two teenage girls, and amputating their arms and legs. He recalls removing healthy kidneys, wombs, livers and still beating hearts to improve his knowledge of anatomy. He said:

> It was educational, and even today when I go to see doctors, they are impressed by my knowledge of the human body. But if I'm really honest, the reason we did it was to take revenge on these people who were spying for the Americans. Now, of course I feel terrible about the

> cruel thing that I did, and I think of it so often. But at the time what I felt for these people was closer to hatred than to pity.

He also talks about a time towards the end of 1944, when he was told by his commanding officer to come and watch a vivisection:

> A middle-aged man had been tied to the bed and had been anaesthetised. The first time it was one prisoner, a middle-aged man. He'd already given up – there was no struggle. He was tied to the bed and anaesthetised with ether, so that he was completely unconscious. The Lieutenant showed me what to do. He cut him open, and pointed out, Here's the liver, here's the kidneys, here's the heart. The heart was still beating, then he cut the heart open and showed me the inside. That was when he died. I didn't want to do it, but it was an order, you see. At that time, if a commander gave you an order it was understood that it was the order of the emperor, and the emperor was a god. I had no choice – if I had disobeyed, I would have been killed. The operation took about an hour; when it was over the body was sewn up and thrown into a hole in the earth.

Makino made frequent visits to San Fernando after the war ended to try to ease his guilty conscience, setting up war memorials in the town, donating clothes to charities and providing the local baseball team with uniforms.

In early 1945, the Japanese knew that they were going to lose the war and that the Philippines would soon be retaken by the Americans. General Yamashita then told his troops: 'Carry out resistance in perpetuity to provide assistance to the never-ending Imperial Fortune by turning yourselves into human pillars, unperturbed, for the Imperial Nation.'

With the Americans closing in on the islands, Japanese troops embarked on an orgy of mass murder. At Port Santiago in Manila, they crammed civilians into cells, tortured them and burned them alive. One Japanese soldier wrote in his diary at the time: 'Burned 1,000 guerrillas to death tonight.'

Two hundred others were locked in a room in St Paul's College; grenades were placed in the chandeliers above the tables and exploded. Those who survived and tried to escape were killed by machine-gun and rifle fire.

On 10 February 1945, around 800 people, including Spanish Filipinos and some German nationals, were crowded into the German club on San Luis

Street in Ermita. A platoon of Japanese troops surrounded the buildings and began to murder everyone there. Edgar Krohn Jr., a Philippine-born German who survived the massacre, tells the story of what happened on that fateful day:

> At about noon, a platoon of Japanese Marines who had cordoned off the 4,000 square meters of the club premises, started killing everyone in sight. The Marines then systematically fired their weapons into the area beneath the club building which had been converted into an emergency air raid shelter. Gasoline was poured into the shelter, and it was torched right after. Those who attempted to escape the inferno were gunned down. Only ten people survived the massacre.

With the end of the war in sight, the Japanese set about destroying the city of Manila, setting fire to homes and killing thousands of men, women and children. Many Filipino women were raped, their small children flung into the air and stabbed with bayonets. In the hospitals, doctors and patients were bayoneted, whilst priests and nuns were hanged in their churches. At one church, Filipino civilians had their heads cut off. An eyewitness gave an account of an atrocity in Manila where he saw his houseboy tied up and had his penis slashed off and shoved in his mouth.

In the hours before the Americans retook Manila in March 1945, Japanese troops took around 100 Filipino guerrillas and their families into a field, where they proceeded to behead the men whilst the women and children were bayoneted. The Japanese seemed intent on destroying the city of Manila and annihilating its inhabitants before they themselves were killed. A document was discovered after the war that gave orders for their troops to murder and burn at random, its wording was:

> Be careful to make no mistakes in the time of exploding and burning when the enemy invades. When killing Filipinos, assemble them together in one place as far as possible, thereby saving ammunition and labour. Disposal of the dead bodies will be troublesome, so either assemble them in houses scheduled to be burned or blown up.

In the town of Luzon, some 200 miles north of Manila, fourteen Filipino resistance fighters were taken prisoner after they had run out of ammunition.

After being made to dig trenches, the first group were pushed into them while still alive. Their colleagues, at bayonet point, were forced to shovel the earth back on top of them, stamping on it until only the head and neck of each man was showing. The last group of prisoners were then shot as the men who had been buried up to their necks looked on in horror. Some of the Japanese soldiers defecated onto banana leaves and as the helpless men were unable to move, had to endure the revolting offerings being shoved into their mouths. The Japanese soldiers laughed and joked with each other as they then proceeded to behead the men.

As the Americans closed in, the Japanese thrust women and children into their front lines to try to protect their positions; any who survived were simply murdered. By now, their command structure had broken down and many of the Japanese troops simply took their frustrations out on the women and children. Catholic priests and nuns were murdered at the De La Salle College on 12 February 1945. About twenty Japanese soldiers stormed through the gates of the college, killing forty-one civilians, including women and young girls. Victims were either shot, slashed, or bayoneted. One woman called Gloria Carlos Vera survived the massacre by pretending to be dead after she was bayoneted in the back by a Japanese soldier.

When US troops entered Manila, they found a city of complete devastation, littered with the bodies of thousands of civilians. A local newspaper wrote after the war:

> The devastation of Manila was one of the great tragedies of the Second World War. Seventy percent of the utilities, seventy-two percent of the factories, eighty percent of the southern residential district, and 100 percent of the business district were razed. Hospitals were set afire after their patients had been strapped to their beds. The corpses of males were mutilated, females of all ages were raped before they were slain, and babies' eyeballs gouged out and smeared on walls like jelly.

When the war ended in August 1955, Lieutenant General Masaharu Homma was put on trial for war crimes in the Philippines. He pleaded guilty as commander but testified that he did not know about them until after they had occurred. He was found guilty for the actions of his troops and executed, despite his wife appealing to American General Douglas MacArthur to spare his life. Rear Admiral Sanji Iwabuchi, who presided over some of the most barbaric massacres of the war, committed suicide rather than surrender;

his body was never found. General Yamashita was also found guilty of war crimes in the Philippines.

In Tokyo, on 3 September 1945, Colonel Sidney Mashbir, the US Army's chief translator, met with Okazaki Katsuo of Japan's Ministry of Foreign Affairs. Mashbir showed him copies of Japanese military orders to burn to death Filipino men, women and children, along with photographs of the horrors of the atrocities in Manila. Visibly disturbed, Okazaki asked Mashbir if the United States had the names of the Japanese soldiers responsible for the atrocities.

'You're damn right,' replied Mashbir. 'Depend on it: you will very shortly be called upon to turn them over to us for punishment.'

Chapter 4

The Hong Kong Massacres

December 1941

On 8 December 1941, within a matter of hours after they had bombed Pearl Harbor and invaded Malaya, the Imperial Japanese Army attacked the British Colony of Hong Kong. At around 2000 hrs that evening, Japanese troops crossed the border from China and engaged the defending Allied troops at Gin Drinkers Lane, a military defensive line near Kwai Chung in the New Territories. As the Allies were vastly outnumbered by the Japanese as they advanced southwards along the Kowloon Peninsula, Major General Christopher Michael Maltby, officer in charge of the Allied forces, had no choice but to order all his troops back to Hong Kong Island.

With Kowloon now under their control, Japanese troops crossed onto Hong Kong Island on 15 December, and within five days had control of more than half of the island, including the main reservoir. Even with the water supply situation now becoming critical, Major General Maltby still would not surrender. Ten days later, on Christmas Day 1941, the Governor General of Hong Kong, Sir Mark Aitchison Young, had no choice but to surrender as Maltby's forces were surrounded, and the population was running out of water.

The Japanese invaders poured into the heavily populated city, where, drunk on alcohol and the drugs of victory, they embarked on a frenzy of killing and raping. At Eucliffe, near Repulse Bay, more than fifty Allied prisoners were bayoneted and beheaded, their bodies simply flung into the sea. Company Sergeant Major Hanlon of the Royal Regiment of Canada was one of only a few who survived. After the war, he told war crimes investigators:

> We knew we were going to be shot because on top of the bank were already pools of blood and at the bottom of the cliff, near the sea, were dozens of dead bodies. It was evident that they had been shot on the

> top of the cliff and had fallen down. Owing to the fact that I turned my head to the left as I was being fired at, the bullet passed through my neck above the left shoulder and came out at my right cheek. I did not lose consciousness and the force of the bullet hitting me knocked me free of the others and I rolled down the cliff. Three others fell on top of me all dead.

As the Japanese troops moved south through the city, they took over the Maryknoll Fathers Mission in Stanley to use as their headquarters. The priests were ordered to line up in the hall and had their cassocks removed, before being tied together in pairs and marched down into the village along with a group of British soldiers. Fifteen of the soldiers were taken away and shot. The remaining soldiers were then herded into a garage, where they were tortured for three days. One British officer was tied up so tightly that he strangled himself, another's tongue was cut out, whilst others had their eyes poked out. Not one soldier from this group survived, but the priests were spared to tell their grim tale at the end of the war.

One of the priests on that fateful day was Father Bernard Tohill, an Irishman from Belfast, very close to my own hometown. Let me digress here. A couple of years ago, my son, who lives in Oxford, was chatting to one of his neighbours called John Tohill. The fact that my son's grandfather had been a Far East prisoner of war came up in the conversation, and that I had written four books on the subject. John casually said that his uncle had also been a Far East prisoner of war. As the conversation progressed, John said that his uncle, Bernard Tohill, had been a priest in Hong Kong when the Japanese invaded the island and was then taken prisoner, where he remained for the rest of the war. John knew very little about his uncle's story and via my son, asked me if I could find out anything about his time as a prisoner of war. I contacted Tony Banham, an expert on Hong Kong during the Second World War and who has written several books on the subject. Tony came back to me quite quickly and told me that he had access to copies of Father Bernard Tohill's diaries and that he would send them on to me. When I received them a few weeks later, I passed them on to John Tohill, who was absolutely delighted to get them.

This is Father Bernard Tohill's account of that fateful day, taken from his diaries kept at the time:

> As time passed and the long squat was dampening our spirits, the officers were convinced that this was the end for them. They expected to be executed. We tried hard to keep their spirits. The ropes that bound them were almost choking them; and we did not dare to loosen them. One Japanese soldier did try, unobtrusively, to help them a little. Some of the priests lit and passed on to them cigarettes.
>
> We were all searched several times and, eventually, tied up in fours, fives or sixes, according to the length of the rope. Altogether we were about thirty-three persons, a Polish Salesian priest, a white Russian, an Australian, a Canadian Passionist Bishop and a Canadian Scarboro Father, two American Passionists, an American Vincentian, an Irish Salesian, and the rest Maryknollers. Father Szeliga, with his little beard, seemed to enjoy the esteem of the soldiers. He was not even tied up, as we were; perhaps the Shanghai identity card he had with him, written in Japanese, won for him a little consideration. The white Russian was not tied up either. But everyone else in the group was. Some thought we were soldiers in disguise and should be liquidated, while others held that the majority of us looked too old to be military personnel. The four British officers squatting with us were grilled; someone tried to cut off their shoulder straps with a sword or bayonet; an order was given for them to get up and move down to the end of the row, where they were brutally bayoneted to death, and this on Christmas morning, right outside the Carmelite Monastery! We were sickened and disgusted; but they bravely faced death. I remember one of the execution squad picking up a piece of paper to wipe clean his bayonet. Later I came to know that Brother Cheung and our boys had been ordered to bury them, and other victims, close by.

At Saint Stephen's College, Tung Tau Wan Road, Stanley, a 400-bed military hospital, containing around 160 wounded Allied soldiers, a Christmas Day party was the last thing on the minds of the staff and patients. On Christmas Eve, the college buildings came under fire from the Japanese invaders, and on Christmas morning at around 0600 hrs, a patrol of around 200 drunken Japanese soldiers approached the building shouting and screaming. Hearing the commotion outside, the head of the hospital, Lieutenant Colonel George Black, went to the main door to confront the mob. Standing in the doorway and pointing to his Red Cross brassard, he shouted: 'You can't come in here this is a hospital.' One of the Japanese soldiers promptly raised his rifle and shot the doctor in the head at point-blank range, leaving him lying on the steps in a pool of blood. The Japanese troops then poured forward into the building, bayoneting Black's dead body as they ran past into the wards, where they ripped the bandages from wounded soldiers and plunged bayonets into open wounds.

A group of St John Ambulance Brigade men who had been tending to patients were herded into a small room, and brutally murdered, only one surviving to tell what happened on that fateful Christmas Day. Within half an hour, almost sixty wounded soldiers lost their lives. Eighty-six other walking wounded, along with several staff, were crammed into a small room, where they were packed so tightly that they were unable to lie down. For the next twenty-four hours, these injured men were not given any food or water. A Canadian Army chaplain called James Barrett saw Japanese soldiers push all the patients and staff who could walk into this small room. And when he heard screaming coming from the room, he decided to investigate. On entering, he saw the most appalling sight: bodies lay on the floor with ears, tongues, noses, and eyes scattered around. Barrett felt sick to the pit of his stomach and at the war crimes tribunals after the war, he gave the following account of what he saw that day:

> After we had been there for about an hour the Japanese moved us up to a smaller room. Until then the nurses had been with me, but as we were being moved from the storeroom to the smaller room they were taken away. I saw one of them beaten over the head with a steel helmet, kicked, and then slapped in the face by a Japanese soldier. In the small room ninety men were placed with me, some of the hospital staff and some of the wounded men. The room was so small that we could not have all sat down together, and it was necessary for the very sick or wounded men to lie down as best they could and when they could. After we had been in the room a little while a Japanese soldier came to the door, made us put up our hands and took my watch, my ring, and some money which I had in my pocket. Later, another Japanese soldier entered with a sack of ammunition and threw cartridges in our faces. Yet a third came in, a few minutes later, and removed two riflemen. Immediately afterwards we heard screams coming from the corridor outside. We remained in this room until 1600 hrs when a Japanese

> soldier entered and gave us to understand by sign language that Hong Kong had surrendered. The next day I made a tour of the hospital. It was in a dreadful state. About seventy or more wounded men had been killed by bayonets while in their beds. Many more were seriously wounded. None of the victims had been armed, nor was the hospital anywhere near the battle area. There were no armed troops or battle positions in the vicinity. I found the dead bodies of the commanding officer of the hospital, and his adjutant, on the ground floor. They had been badly mutilated.

Four female nurses from the hospital were gang-raped while lying on top of the dead bodies of some of the soldiers, before they themselves were taken into the grounds and murdered.

One of the soldiers recuperating in the hospital at the time was Colour Sergeant S.D. Begg of the Hong Kong Volunteer Defence Corps. Begg's wife was a nurse in the hospital and the couple were happy that they had both survived the initial massacre, but unfortunately, the following day his wife and two other nurses were found murdered.

Another survivor of the massacre, Sergeant John Herbert Anderson of the RAMC, made this statement after the war:

> The SJAB [St John Ambulance] men were all put in one room and systematically butchered, one only remained alive to tell us what happened. Eighty-six patients and staff including myself were locked in a small room. During the day at intervals, parties of Japanese came along and peered in at us, on most occasions seizing one of the men and dragging him out to the corridor. The bodies of four of these men were afterwards found bayoneted and tortured and sounds of this going on could be heard in the corridor. The bodies of three missing women including Mrs Begg were found in the grounds covered by a blanket. They had been cut to pieces – Mrs Begg's head was almost severed from her body. Altogether about sixty to seventy bodies of patients and twenty-five of staff were collected. Under orders from the Japanese a huge bonfire was built for the burning of the bodies.

Another survivor, nursing sister Miss Amelia Fleming Gordon of the Territorial Army Nursing Service, gave this statement:

> Around 0900 hrs on Christmas morning we were marched in single file upstairs into a small room – dead bodies and blood covered the stairs – and at the top of the landing several Japs hit us as we passed. We were then put into different classrooms, I was going into a small room with four VADs (Mrs Smith, Mrs Begg, Mrs Buxton, and Mrs Simmons) where there were five Chinese women (wives of British soldiers). We remained here all day. A particularly bad lot of Japanese soldiers (five in all) came in at 1630 hrs and removed Mrs Smith, Begg and Buxton – these three we never saw again. I was taken to another room, where there were two dead bodies, and made to take off all my clothes whilst they removed theirs. Before touching me they apparently became afraid someone was coming and made me put my clothes on again and I was returned to the room. We were left in peace for a short time only – three soldiers came in and took me to a small adjacent bathroom, knocked me down and all raped me one after the other, and then let me return. Mrs Fidoe was then taken and underwent a similar experience. Both Mrs Fidoe and I were then taken out a second time and raped as before.

Atrocities were carried out by Japanese soldiers throughout Hong Kong. Many incidents of rape were reported on thousands of women and young girls, with others forced into prostitution. Some of the female population managed to avoid the Japanese soldiers by dressing in filthy clothes; others shaved their heads or wore men's clothes.

Ramón Lavalle, a young Argentinean consular staff member based in Hong Kong at the time, on being made aware of Japanese troops entering the Kowloon hospital and demanding women for sex, reported this to the Japanese military authorities. He requested that they be protected from further exploitation, but it was simply refused by Colonel Nishiyama, who said: 'I cannot spare the soldiers to protect the enemy and that moreover it was not logical to appreciate the needs of the soldiers and that the soldiers were soldiers not angels.'

Whilst the citizens of Hong Kong endured a reign of terror during the Japanese occupation there were many heroic acts carried out, and one in particular stands out. Several seriously injured Allied soldiers were being looked after in a hotel at Shallow Water Bay, when a patrol of Japanese soldiers arrived and were about to take them outside to kill them. A foreign nurse stepped in front and said, 'If you want to kill them, you have to kill me first.' The Japanese soldiers quickly retreated.

As the war drew to a close in 1945, the Japanese continued to terrorise the population of Hong Kong, and indeed carried on even after Japan had surrendered. From 16 to 26 August, a small garrison of Japanese soldiers in Silver Ore Bay on Lantau Island (where the new Hong Kong international airport is currently located) went on the rampage, slaughtering, robbing and burning to the ground several small villages.

There were many heroes during this time, including Colonel Lance Newnham of the Middlesex Regiment, Captain Douglas Ford of the Royal Scots, and Flight Lieutenant Hector Bertram Gray of the Royal Air Force. The three men were planning a mass escape by British forces but were captured and tortured. They were forced to dig their own graves, before being executed by Japanese firing squad at Sham Shui on 18 December 1943. The three men are buried in Stanley Prison cemetery. All three were posthumously awarded the George Cross for their gallantry.

During the three years and eight months of Japanese occupation of Hong Kong, it is estimated that 10,000 civilians were executed, whilst many others were tortured, raped, or mutilated. Estimates for Allied military casualties are 1,111 killed, 1,167 missing and 1,362 wounded.

Chapter 5

The Singapore Chinese Massacre (Sook Ching)

February 1942

A mighty Island Fortress, the guardian of the East
An up-to-date Gibraltar, a thousand planes at least
It simply can't be taken twill stand a siege for years
We can hold the place forever, and bring our foe to tears
Our men are there in million. The defences are unique
But the Japs did not believe you, so they took it in a week.
(Written by an anonymous British soldier)

When Singapore fell to the Japanese on 15 February 1942, the city's 800,000 Chinese population, most of whom were anti-Japanese, became very concerned about how they would be treated. They were aware of the savage acts of brutality that had been carried out in their Chinese homelands over the previous ten years and they felt the same thing might happen to them.

General Tomoyuki Yamashita, commander of the Japanese forces, worried that the large Chinese population might rise up and revolt, appointed Major General Kawamura Saburō, a notorious disciplinarian, to be in charge of the Singapore garrison. The Japanese high command issued a directive making it clear that all anti-Japanese elements on the island were to be targeted and eliminated. It highlighted five separate categories against which action was to be taken:

1. Former members of volunteer forces.
2. Communists.
3. Looters.
4. Armed people of those found to be harbouring guns.
5. Anyone obstructing the Japanese operation or threatening law and order.

Saburō's first action to try to eradicate the threat was to register the Chinese population. He was also concerned about the members of Dalforce, a Chinese regiment that fought against the Japanese in the battle for Singapore, many of whom disappeared back into the population when the island fell.

On 18 February, all Chinese males between the ages of 16 and 50 were ordered to report to twenty-eight mass screening centres across the city. Any refusal resulted in severe punishment for disobedience; in fact, this meant they would be executed. The Chinese people were terrified. 'What is going to happen to us?' was the question on everyone's lips. Many went into hiding when Japanese troops began to search the houses for young Chinese who had not reported. A Japanese sergeant called Yamaguchi said to the Chinese people at one registration centre:

> While building a road, if a tree is found to be causing an obstruction, not only is it cut down, but its roots are removed so that it would not grow again. The same would apply to a person who was guilty of a serious crime against the Japanese. Not only would he be removed, but also his roots, meaning his family and close friends. So, you see, it is necessary to purify the population and get rid of evil. The Japanese army was forced to carry out such purification methods in China against the enemies of Japan who had refused to co-operate with the Japanese authorities. If the Chinese people in Singapore also adopt this attitude, they too will be exterminated.

This was a blatant warning to the Chinese people of Singapore that they would be brutally treated if they did not follow the rules of the occupying forces.

At the screening centres, they were told to write down their names. Some wrote their names in English and some in Chinese. Anyone writing their name in English was classified as pro-British. For several days, they were detained, checked and given identification stamps on their shirts, arms or singlets. At one screening station in Jalan Besar stadium, people were marched past a Japanese officer who, if he raised his left hand as a person passed him, that person was to be arrested; if he raised his right hand, the person was free to go. The lives of many Chinese people in Singapore were dependant on the whim of a Japanese officer.

After screening, anyone who was deemed to be anti-Japanese was taken to the Tanjong Wharves to be shot or beheaded. Others were taken out in boats on the river, pushed overboard and shot as they tried to swim away. Around 800 Chinese people from the Jalan Besar area were taken to a village on the east coast and brutally murdered, closely followed by another group at Tanaka Merah Besar beach further along the coast. A Chinese man called Wong Peng Yin, who managed to survive these murders, recalled later:

> When we got off the lorries the Japanese guards tied us in fives, and we were marched down to the beach. When we got there, I noticed some dead bodies lying there, they were all Chinese. As soon as I got into the water my rope loosened and then we were marched into the sea. The Japanese guards who had remained on the beach opened fire with machine guns and rifles. I managed to struggle out of my ropes and swim away in the direction of Mata Ikan village where I waded ashore and spent the night in a squatter's house. As far as I know only one other in my group escaped and he was wounded.

Another survivor, Chua Choon Guan, who had been taken to a beach at Tanah Merah, also recalled the horrors:

> Everyone else died because I never saw them again. I was in the fifth row to be machine-gunned. The bullets hit me, but I was not killed. I fell and the others who were shot dead fell on top of me. I was almost unconscious and then I felt a hard blow on my head that made me completely unconscious. When I regained consciousness, it was dark. I had come to because the waves lapped against my face. I was still bound but I found a sharp rock near the beach and was able to cut the rope by rubbing it against the rock. I then crawled away and escaped.

The lorries that took these men to the beaches passed through the British prisoner of war camp at Changi, and the troops there suspected that the Chinese were being taken to be executed. A little later, they heard the chatter of machine-gun fire coming from the direction of the beach and their thoughts were confirmed. They had been ordered to stay away from that section of the beach where they usually went for a swim.

One of the British prisoners in Changi at the time, a Doctor Roy, was informed by a Malay fisherman there had been four survivors of the shooting on the beach. The following morning, Roy went back to the beach with Sergeant B.W. Brown of the East Surrey Regiment (Sergeant Brown's son is a very good friend of mine), where a group of British prisoners were burying the bodies. He discovered a badly wounded Chinese man in the long grass and managed to take him to the 198 Field Ambulance unit. A little later, he found another two Chinese men who were also badly wounded.

On 23 February, several lorries loaded with Chinese civilians were spotted near Ponggol beach on the east of the island. A Singaporean man said that he watched the Japanese guards escort them down onto the beach, force them to kneel at the water's edge and then shoot them. The few who survived the shooting were bayoneted or beheaded.

A plaque was erected on the beach by the National Heritage Board of Singapore, and it reads:

> On 23 February 1942, some 300 to 400 Chinese civilians were killed along the Ponggol foreshore by *'hojo kempei'* Japanese military police firing squad. They were among tens of thousands who lost their lives during the Japanese *'Sook Ching'* operation to purge suspected anti-Japanese civilians among Singapore's Chinese population between 18 February and 4 March 1942. The victims who perished along the foreshore were among 1,000 Chinese males rounded up following a house-to-house search of the Chinese community living along Upper Serangoon Road, by Japanese soldiers.

In another massacre, 700 Chinese were taken to an area just east of Changi and decapitated, their headless bodies slung into mass graves, their heads piled into the back of a lorry and taken away. The following day, Singaporeans were astonished to see these heads mounted on long bamboo stakes around the city. An angry waitress in a Singapore restaurant asked the Japanese officers: 'Are there any courts in Japan? Are people condemned to death under Japanese law? Do you stick decapitated heads up on the streets of Tokyo?'

One Chinese man recalled that he saw a woman's corpse with a bamboo pole stuck into her genitals. Mothers shaved the heads of their daughters before dressing them in boys' clothes, in a desperate attempt to ensure that they would not be raped or become sex slaves in brothels run by the Japanese. The *Syonan Times*, a newspaper now controlled by the Japanese, reported on 23 February a veiled threat that:

> It is hereby declared that the recent arrests of hostile and rebellious Chinese have drastically been carried out in order to establish the prompt

> restoration of the peace and also to establish the new bright Malaya. Any Chinese who have hitherto been in sympathy with propaganda of Chungking government, and have positively participated in the British Army, in forming volunteer corps and still have secretly disturbed the military activities of the Nippon army as guerrilla corps or spies are indeed so-called traitors of the East Asia, disturbing the establishment of the Greater East Asia. Thus, it is most important to sweep away these treacherous Chinese elements and to establish the peace and welfare of the populace.

One Japanese officer, Lieutenant Colonel Masayuki, said at his war crimes trial that Colonel Tsuji had told him that the intention was to kill half the Chinese population of Singapore. One Japanese officer in Singapore, after its capitulation, was heard to say: 'We hated and despised the Chinese more than we did the Americans or the British.'

It has been estimated that 6,000 Chinese people were killed in what was termed by the Japanese as 'Operation Clean Up', but some people maintain that it could have been more like 50,000. Construction workers in Singapore were still coming across bones up until the 1980s.

As well as many accounts by Chinese survivors, there were also some by British gunners who were hiding out on Blakang Mati island (now Sentosa Island). They testified that they saw a tugboat firing at the bodies of Chinese floating off Keppel Harbour. British civilian prisoners of war in Changi gaol also testified to the murders. Some of them, charged with burying bodies, managed to rescue a few wounded Chinese, and hide them in the hospital.

A Japanese war historian called Iwaichi Fujiwara was reported as saying after the war:

> There was no room for the Japanese army to counter-argue the charge of the inhumane murders in which countless Chinese were executed indiscriminately on the beaches, in rubber plantations and in the jungles without investigations or trials. There was no justification for the massacres, even if some Chinese had fought us as volunteers and collaborated with anti-Japanese elements.

For many years, the Chinese population of Singapore bore an intense hatred of the Japanese military for the terrors and atrocities wrought on them during the Sook Ching purge.

Chapter 6

The Bangka Island Massacre

12–14 February 1942

On 12 February 1942, with Singapore only hours away from falling to the Japanese forces, sixty-five Australian Army nurses of the 2/10th and the 2/13th Australian General Hospitals in Singapore, together with a group of injured soldiers and 116 other civilian women and children, boarded the liner SS *Vyner Brooke* in Keppel Harbour. Under the command of Matrons Paschke and Drummond, the sixty-five Australian nurses were briefed as to their duties in the event of a sinking. News of the atrocities carried out in the St Stephen's hospital in Hong Kong (see Chapter 4) had filtered through to Singapore and the authorities were worried that nurses in the city might face the same fate if they remained.

Captained by R.E. Borton, OBE, the *Vyner Brooke* was to take the nurses and civilians to the safety of Java, which was still under Dutch control. As it usually only carried twelve passengers in addition to a crew of forty-seven, the ship was crowded and sat low in the water.

The *Vyner Brooke* left the mayhem of Singapore as dusk fell and headed out of Keppel Harbour into the South China Sea. The passengers looked back towards Singapore with a heavy heart as bombs dropped on the city and flames licked up into the evening sky. They all prayed for their friends and relatives left on the island.

As dawn broke the following morning, the ship laid up in the lee of a small jungle-covered island, where it lay at anchor until late in the afternoon. At around 1600 hrs, as the crew prepared to depart, the tranquilly on board was shattered when it was attacked by Japanese dive-bombers. Fortunately, the bombs missed, and Captain Borton decided to make a run for the Bangka Strait towards Palembang in Sumatra.

The night of the 13th was uneventful, but by daylight on the 14th, the ship was dangerously exposed on a flat sea just inside the strait. There was no sign of any Japanese ships or aircraft, but their luck was not to last as the

Vyner Brooke was soon to be attacked by several Japanese aircraft. One bomb hit the bridge, with another going right down the funnel into the engine room, and within fifteen minutes, the ship had disappeared below the waves. After the war, Betty Jeffrey, one of the nurses on board, outlined the sinking:

> Sister Ennis and I made a beeline for the bridge. … we were told to see that every civilian person was to be off the ship before leaving it ourselves. Believe me we didn't waste time getting overboard. But the planes had not finished with us. Over they came again and machined-gunned the deck and all the lifeboats. Two dropped into the sea, one filled and sank, the other turned upside down and drifted away. The third was already manned by two sailors and I'm sure they never anticipated such a quick trip down. … at this stage there were quite a few people in the water and the ship was listing heavily to starboard, two boats got away safely.

Two of the nurses, Vivian Bullwinkel and Kath Neuss, managed to clamber into a lifeboat as dead bodies floated around them. The lifeboats were strafed by the Japanese aircraft, but the pair managed to reach Bangka Island off the coast of Sumatra. Twelve of the Australian nurses were either killed in the attack on the ship or drowned in the sea.

Around 100 of the nurses and civilians reached the island, where they were washed up on Radji Beach. As they waded ashore, they were met by some of the local people who advised them to give themselves up to the Japanese. After discussing their options, it was decided that those who were fit enough should walk to the nearest Japanese camp and give themselves up, whilst the injured and ill were to remain on the beach. Some of the nurses, including Vivien Bullwinkel and Kath Neuss, volunteered to stay with the injured.

A few hours later, a Japanese platoon of about twelve men marched onto the beach, where the injured soldiers and the nurses were sitting. Unfortunately, the soldiers were from the Orita Battalion, the battalion that had carried out the murder and rapes that had taken place in Hong Kong a few months earlier, identified by the gold balls on their uniforms. (See Chapter 4.)

They proceeded to separate the men from the women and drag them around a headland out of sight of the nurses. Vivian Bullwinkel tells what happened next:

> All the injured men who were still there, which would have been about fifty or sixty, were rounded up and taken around the bluff, and when they [the Japanese] came back some little time later they were wiping their bayonets, so we looked at each other and said, 'they're not taking prisoners.'

One of the men who survived this massacre, Ernie Lloyd, wrote after the war:

> The man next to me, Jock McGurk said 'this is where you get it Ernie, right in the back' I said, not for me Jock, and we both dived into the sea, with one other man, as the Japs opened fire with a machine gun. They mowed down the others first and then turned the gun on the three of us. I was a powerful swimmer and was going well. Jock cried out. 'Ernie, I'm hit' and both he and the other man sank out of sight. I then got the Japs' undivided attention – and they weren't going to leave anyone alive. I saw a bullet hit the water at my side and then felt a bullet hit my head and I thought it had gone right through; but in fact it only grazed my scalp. Then another bullet went right through my left shoulder and leg. I must have looked – and certainly felt – a dead man as I floated half submerged round the rocks, was washed up on a bit of sand, and lost consciousness.

A US citizen called Eric Germann, who was on the *Vyner Brooke*, also witnessed this massacre. He saw the Japanese take the first group of eight men, including Ernie Lloyd, along the beach, over a small promontory of rocks and driftwood about 200 feet away, where they were murdered. He was in the next group who were then ordered to march the same route and face the sea. The next thing Germann knew, he was face down in the sea and in pain – he played for dead. After some time, he could see the Japanese had left him, but he continued to lie still, and then ran up the beach and into the jungle, and then south about a mile until he found a small stream running into the sea, where he hid and rested. He had been bayoneted through the chest. The following day, he continued further south and came across some Malay fishermen who took him to Muntok, where he was interned in the cinema.

When the Japanese soldiers came back to where the remaining twenty-two nurses, along with one civilian woman, were sat on the beach waiting in terror, they knew what was coming next. One of the nurses, Sister Elaine

Balfour-Ogilvy, suggested that the nurses all run in different directions so that at least some of them would survive. This idea was overruled by Matron Drummond, who told them they must all comply with Japanese instructions to avoid letting their wounded patients down.

At bayonet point and still wearing their grey dresses and Red Cross armbands, they were forced to wade out into the sea. As they did, one of the nurses, Alma Beard, turned and said to her friend, 'The two things I hate most are the Japs and the sea – and I've got them both.' Bullwinkel goes on to say:

> They then machine-gunned us from behind. I was hit just in the back there, and it came out here. And being very young and naive I suppose I always thought that once you were shot, you know you'd had it. And really to my utter amazement I found that I was still alive, and then of course I became frightened. I had taken in a lot of salt water therefore I was being horribly seasick, and I thought, oh they'll see my shoulders moving, so then I tried to stop being seasick, but – and I just lay there, because well, I was too frightened to do anything else, and then gradually the waves brought me back to the beach. And I finally plucked up enough courage to sit up and look around and there is no sign of my colleagues, the Japanese party had gone, and there was just, you know, the usual travel brochure of blue sky, palms and golden sands. I lay there for ten minutes, and everything seemed quiet, I sat up and looked around and there was no sign of anybody. Then I got up and went into the jungle and lay down and either slept or was unconscious for a couple of days.

(It was not until many years later that it was discovered that the nurses had been raped before they were shot. Vivian Bullwinkel had kept this to herself before disclosing it in an interview with ABC journalist Tess Lawrence, and also to a retired Major Hinks, in the 1990s. This is backed up by an examination of Sister Bullwinkel's uniform, which disclosed that her uniform would have been pulled up and undone for the bullet holes in the front and back to have matched. It was also supported by evidence that bodies were found above the tideline; some were naked and had severe head injuries. Again, evidence came to light that some of the nurses were restrained by manacles in a nearby fisherman's hut.)

Desperately thirsty, sister Bullwinkel eventually crawled back to near the beach, where she found a freshwater spring to slake her thirst. As she lay beside the spring, thanking God for her survival, she heard a male voice call out to her; it was the only other survivor of the massacre, a wounded British Army private called Cecil Kinsley. Kinsley had been bayoneted twice while lying on a stretcher, but fortunately the bayonet had not penetrated any of his vital organs. He feigned dead before crawling away into the jungle after the Japanese had left.

Vivian Bullwinkel takes up the story again:

> On my way to a freshwater spring that was there, somebody spoke to me. On looking round, I saw that it was one of the English soldiers who had joined us on the Sunday night. He was one of the stretcher cases and he had been bayoneted by the same party of Japanese that had shot the girls on Monday morning. All the other stretcher cases had likewise been bayoneted and left for dead.

For the next ten days, Bullwinkel and Kinsley hid in the jungle, surviving off fruits and water from a stream and scrounging food from a nearby village. When they felt they were strong enough, they decided to walk towards Muntok, a distance of around 5 miles. As they stumbled along, on 28 February they were picked up by a Japanese officer in a passing car and taken to a nearby prisoner of war camp in Muntok. Kinsley was then transferred to a men's prisoner of war camp, where he died from his wounds shortly afterwards.

One of the other nurses to be brutally murdered was Sister Clare Halligan. During the bombing of the ship, she was badly injured by a bomb blast, suffering deep shrapnel wounds to the back of her thighs and buttocks, wounds that penetrated to the bone.

Despite being in shock and bleeding profusely, she was helped by fellow nurses up to the deck and into a lifeboat. However, it overturned as it hit the sea, throwing most of its passengers out. Sister Halligan managed to hold on to the upturned craft and – in what must have been excruciating pain – endured many hours before being washed up at one end of Radji Beach, where she was massacred along with the other nurses. Thus ended the life of a woman in her prime, whose life had been dedicated to caring for others in pain and suffering.

In the camp she was taken to in Muntok, Vivian Bullwinkel met up with the other thirty-two nurses who had survived out of the original sixty-five who had left Singapore on the *Vyner Brooke*. In the camp, Sister Bullwinkel covered her wounds with canteens so that she would not be accused of surviving the massacre on the beach. One of the sisters in the camp, Margot Turner, quickly realised that she was keeping something to herself, and recalled: 'She walked quietly in through the door of the jail, clasping an army water bottle to her side. We could see at once why she was doing this – to hide a bullet hole in her uniform.'

Anxious to keep her nightmare experience to herself, she was concerned that if the Japanese found out, they would kill her, as she was the only witness to the slaughter, but naturally the other nurses wanted to hear about her experience. She relented on the understanding that they would keep it to themselves, and it would never be mentioned again.

Out of the sixty-five nurses who left Singapore on the *Vyner Brooke*, twelve drowned, twenty-one were massacred in the water at Radji Beach and thirty-two were taken to a prisoner of war camp near Palembang in southern Sumatra. There they were to spend the next three and a half years, enduring privation and punishment as prisoners of war.

One of the most puzzling things to come out about the massacres was that the Japanese left the soldiers' bodies on the beach, whereas the nurses were driven into the sea and machine-gunned as a group. They wanted to ensure there was no evidence left of the women's bodies, as the officer of the Japanese would have been well aware that he was violating the Geneva Convention by killing the nurses, whilst he could claim that the soldiers were killed in action.

After the war, when the Japanese were pleading for clemency, an article in the Australian *Women's Weekly* magazine appeared, which said:

> If ever, anywhere in the world, a plea for mercy or leniency for the Japanese race is heard, there will rise before Australian eyes the accusing picture of twenty-two gallant women, walking with heads held high into the sea as the Japanese machine guns opened their murderous fire.

After the war ended, the Japanese officer in charge at the time of the Bangka Island Massacre, Captain Orita, was found to be in Russian hands and was handed over to the Australians in Tokyo. He was arrested and put on trial for the atrocity, but committed suicide in his cell in Sugamo Prison on 11 August 1948.

In 1992, Vivian Bullwinkel returned to Bangka Island to unveil a memorial to the nurses who were killed on the *Vyner Brooke*, those who died in the sinking, and those who perished in the internment camps of Sumatra. She died in Perth, Australia, in 2000, aged 84.

Chapter 7

The Alexandra Hospital Massacre, Singapore

February 1942

'Japanese soldiers were advancing across the hospital grounds and seconds later all hell broke out downstairs. The Japanese had entered the hospital and gone berserk bayoneting surgeons, nurses, and patients, some of them lying in the operating theatres, I suddenly remembered that I still had the dead Japanese Officer's watch that I had taken from him back at Kampar. I began to panic. God, I thought if they find that on me, I'm definitely dead. I got out of bed as quickly as my aching leg would let me, grabbed the watch, and limped to the toilet at the end of the ward and with great difficulty placed the watch on top of the cistern, and then quickly hobbled back into bed.'

(Lance Corporal John Wyatt,
2nd Battalion East Surrey Regiment)

The Alexandra British military hospital, situated just off the Alexandra Road and adjacent to the main Federated Malay States railway line, was the main military hospital in Singapore during the Japanese invasion in February 1942. Opened on 19 July 1940, it was built in typical colonial style on three storeys, with spacious grounds surrounding the buildings.

On the morning of 13 February 1942 (known as 'black Friday'), Japanese mortar bombs began landing to the front and to the rear of the hospital buildings, even though they were clearly marked by red crosses indicating that it was a medical facility and not a military target. At the same time, ill-directed British mortar shells also began landing near to the front entrance. Two Allied units of the 44th Indian Brigade were deployed very near the hospital, holding a defensive line just to the north. None were inside the hospital compound.

By early afternoon, the shelling had increased dramatically and the hospital commanding officer, Lieutenant Colonel Craven, decided that the chief matron along with her eight nursing sisters should leave the hospital for their own safety and head for the docks. These brave ladies volunteered to stay on despite the risk, but Craven insisted they leave as he had received a cable informing him about atrocities committed by the Japanese to nurses in Saint Stephen's hospital in Hong Kong. (See Chapter 4.)

There were now very few civilian staff left, with the Royal Army Medical Corps staff running all aspects of the administration. The hospital was crammed with around 800 patients, mainly British along with some Indians, Malays and Australians. New casualties were arriving by the lorry load every hour, with around 200 medical staff of 32 Company Royal Army Medical Corps doing a wonderful job under difficult circumstances in tending for the badly injured soldiers. Patients were crammed into wards, with others lying on the floor or in camp beds in the corridors all over the building. Even the dining room had been converted into a temporary ward.

With much of the mains water supply in Singapore damaged by the bombing, water was kept in every available container, including buckets, baths and petrol cans. The electricity supply had also been cut off and operations were being conducted by torch and candlelight. The situation in the hospital was indeed becoming desperate.

As daylight began to fade, the ground floor of the hospital was in chaos; wounded men filled every inch of available space and the 180-strong staff worked tirelessly to try to alleviate the pain of the suffering soldiers. Staff struggled to make their way through the mayhem in the course of their duties and medical supplies were beginning to run out.

The following morning, Japanese bombs again began dropping around the hospital, leaving it meat in a very explosive sandwich.

A patient in the hospital at the time, Corporal John Wyatt of the 2 East Surreys, was awoken just after 0800 hrs that morning by the noise of the heavy bombs landing all around the building. He recalls:

> The shelling went on for most of the morning and it was just before lunchtime when I hobbled across to the window to try to see what was happening. I was stunned by the sight that met my eyes as I gazed out across the grounds. Around 100 heavily armed Japanese soldiers were advancing across the hospital grounds. Seconds later, all hell broke out downstairs and one of the most dreadful, cold-blooded massacres had commenced.
>
> (In an interview with the author in 2012.)

As this initial group of Japanese soldiers approached the sisters' quarters, Captain Bartlett of the Royal Army Medical Corps walked towards them with his arms in the air shouting, 'Hospital, hospital', and pointing to his Red Cross brassard. Ignoring the fact that he was obviously a doctor or a nurse, they fired at him. Fortunately, they missed, and he sprinted back into one of the wards.

Inside the hospital, Lieutenant Colonel Craven was discussing the gravity of the situation with his officer in charge of radiography, Major Bull. The two men were in an upstairs office when a bullet came in through the open window causing them to throw themselves to the floor. After a few minutes, the colonel decided to go downstairs to assess the situation for himself. The scene that greeted him was one of utter carnage. More than fifty patients and staff had been shot or bayoneted and many others had been taken away by the Japanese soldiers.

Some of the patients lying on the floor in the dining room saw soldiers of the 44th Indian Brigade moving swiftly along the corridor from the medical wards, closely pursued by a cluster of Japanese troops. Why the Punjabis were fighting in the hospital, no one knows, but some people believe that the presence of armed troops in and around the hospital inflamed the situation, causing the Japanese to react as they did.

The assault on the hospital was undertaken by a company of about 175 Japanese soldiers dressed in full combat kit consisting of green tropical uniforms, steel helmets, rifles, bayonets, and machine guns. Each man was heavily camouflaged with small branches, twigs and leaves stuck all over his body. They gave the impression to the patients of being either drunk or high on drugs.

One group came in from the adjacent railway line and quickly entered the hospital through the main entrance; a second group came in through the rear entrance and the patients' dining room, with a third entering through the operating rooms' windows and through the surgical wards. Staff in the laboratory who saw the first group coming towards the hospital were tragically cut down by a burst of machine-gun fire while trying to run towards the main building. The officer in charge, Major Calder, was killed, along with Sergeant Williams, but Corporal Saint managed to crawl to the main building with a wounded arm, where Private Sutton attended to him. Two Japanese soldiers entered the temporary ward in the dining room, where over 100 patients were lying on camp beds. One of them started beating the helpless patients with a brush while the other completely humiliated another by urinating on him.

Lieutenant Weston decided to take a white sheet and wave it out of the back door of the hospital, but he was simply bayoneted through the white flag by the first Japanese soldier that reached him. The rest of the soldiers in this group stormed into the room and began shooting and bayoneting many of the helpless patients. Among those killed in this early orgy of violence was Padre Smith of the Gordon Highlanders, Staff Sergeant Walker of the Royal Army Dental Corps and Sergeant Sherriff of the Royal Army Medical Corps.

With the hospital now in a complete state of disarray and panic, many staff and some of the more mobile patients tried to escape from the marauding assassins, some with greater degrees of success than others. Those who tried to escape through the main entrance were simply mowed down by rifle and machine-gun fire, whilst others met their fate in the rear corridor, where they were bayoneted or shot before they had a chance to leave the building. Corporal Collins was bayoneted through the chest but fortunately, it missed his vital organs and he survived. Company Quartermaster Sergeant Hartley was not so fortunate and was the oldest man to die in the massacre, aged 57.

Despite the mayhem, the surgeons tried to carry on with operations in the theatres, but when this proved too dangerous because of stray bullets, they moved patients into the corridors. The sheer dedication and bravery of the medical staff was of the highest order.

One of the doctors, a Captain Smiley, moved over to a doorway and indicated to the red cross clearly displayed on his armband. He then motioned to the Japanese soldiers to come into the theatre to show them that they were not at any risk and that it was indeed simply an operating theatre. One of the soldiers fired at him, but the shot missed and hit Private Lewis, who was assisting him, in the shoulder. Smiley then told the medical team to stand quietly in the centre of the room with their arms in the air, leaving the patient on the operating table. They were then ordered out into the corridor and as they moved along, they were attacked viciously with bayonets and rifle butts. Captain Smiley took a bayonet thrust to his chest, but fortunately he had his metal cigarette case in his pocket and the blade was deflected. He stumbled against Private Sutton and they both fell to the ground, pretending to be dead – an act that probably saved their lives. The patient they had been operating on, Corporal Vetch, was stabbed to death while still under anaesthetic. Perhaps in some respects, he was one of the 'lucky' ones as he would have been completely unaware of the sheer terror around him. Many others in the hospital were not so lucky. Private Rodgers, Captain Parkinson, Corporal McEwan and Lance Corporal Lewis were repeatedly bayoneted, and all died almost immediately.

As Smiley and Sutton lay motionless on the floor, they became aware of a large group of patients and medical staff running along the corridor with their arms raised. The Japanese were kicking and beating them with rifle butts as they stumbled along. Others entered several of the surgical wards and began systematically to beat up the helpless patients, many with fractures who were in plaster casts. They seemed to take great pleasure in twisting and pulling at the slings holding some of the men's broken legs in the air.

In the kitchen adjacent to the surgical wards, two of the medical staff, Private Sayer and Private Bruce, were hiding badly wounded Private Guillim, when another patient burst into the room, bleeding profusely from a bayonet wound. Almost immediately, two Japanese soldiers followed him into the room and shot Private Bruce three times in the abdomen. Guillim lay motionless on the floor in a state of abject terror while this attack was going on. They must have been convinced he was dead because they left the room soon after, leaving him to crawl back to the main ward.

After only about half an hour from the initial assault on the hospital, around fifty staff and patients were dead, with many more lying around in great pain from their wounds. At around 1530 hrs (an hour after the initial assault), over a hundred patients and staff were roped together in groups of eight and forced to walk to a piece of open ground about 100 yards from the main buildings. A second group of around sixty (mainly officers) were taken out to a separate piece of land and roped together.

Many of the patients in the first group were walking wounded with arms in plaster, most in bare feet and dressed in pyjamas; any who had difficulty walking were supported by their comrades. This group was marched alongside the main railway embankment, past the Normanton fuel oil tanks, which were on fire and belching huge clouds of black smoke into the hot and humid air. At one point, they were told to stop and rest, when they had all valuables such as rings, watches and pens removed, before being subjected to beatings with rifle butts and fists. One man whose arm was in plaster had it forced behind his back and re-broken.

The building into which they were forced was a redbrick, two-storey house raised above the ground on piles, with a block of outbuildings surrounding a small courtyard. It was part of the hospital's sisters' quarters and had three very small rooms, each with double doors opening directly onto the courtyard. The patients were crammed so tightly into the rooms that it was impossible for everyone to sit down at the same time. The doors were then secured with wooden poles, and the windows nailed closed and shuttered to prevent any daylight entering. There was no ventilation, and within minutes, the heat had become unbearable. They were crammed in tighter than battery hens and soon had to suffer the indignity of relieving themselves over each other, and of course, the smell soon became appalling.

The Japanese made no effort to provide these unfortunate men with food or drink, and as the conditions under which they were held were so inhumane, many of them became mentally unstable. Some began to shout and scream at the tops of their voices, appealing for food and drink, whilst others just slumped on the floor, giving up the will to live. The screaming and shouting went on all through the night and at one point, a voice was heard from outside the rooms speaking in perfect English: 'If you keep quiet, I will try and get you back to the hospital tomorrow.' Such a promise, however, did little to alleviate their discomfort. Several of the men died during that night – at least seven in the central room alone. The following day, with no sign of any food or water, desperation began to set in amongst the prisoners, until at around 1100 hrs, a Japanese officer opened the door of one of the rooms and announced in broken English: 'We are taking you behind the lines – you will get water on the way.'

A few minutes later, they were removed in twos by the guards, everyone assuming that they were being taken out for a drink, until they heard screams and shouts in English from nearby: 'Oh my god – mother – don't – help me.' It dawned on the remaining prisoners that that they were now being executed, which was confirmed when a returning Japanese soldier was seen wiping blood from his bayonet with a large piece of cloth.

By mid-afternoon, more than half of the men had been taken to meet their fate, but luck was with the men left in one of the rooms when a shell landed nearby, blowing open the doors and windows. Several were injured by the flying debris but those who were able made a dash for freedom – some through the broken door and others through the windows. A few managed to get away but the rest were killed by a burst of machine-gun fire. Among those who escaped through the door and windows were Corporal Bryer, Private Hoskins, Private Gurd, Captain De Warrenne Waller and Corporal Johnson. When Bryer escaped through the doorway, he turned left, skirted around the rear of the building, and ran along Alexandra Road, where he bumped into Hoskins. Both men ran along together, zigzagging to avoid enemy fire, but unfortunately, Bryer was hit in the back and collapsed. 'I'm done for – you go on,' he called out to Hoskins, who, realising that if he hesitated, he too would be a goner, ran on towards a hut on the other side of the road, where an Indian family gave him some water. With the Japanese in the vicinity, he ran on until finally reaching a patrol of the Beds and Herts, who took him to their company headquarters and from there back into Singapore city.

Meanwhile, Bryer, not too badly wounded, was able to get up and try to get away from the area. Unfortunately, he came across a Japanese patrol that stabbed him four times with their bayonets before hitting him on the side of his head, knocking him into a semi-conscious state. Lying on the ground, he pretended to be dead until dusk, when he stumbled on to look for help.

The day after Singapore surrendered, 16 February 1942, Lieutenant General Mutaguchi, commander of the Japanese 18th Division, visited the hospital and made a speech of apology to the staff and surviving patients for the atrocity. He said:

> General Yamashita is apologising for the behaviour of the frontline troops, but they were overexcited, and he apologises for the overexcitement of his frontline troops, but there will be no more Japanese in the hospital. He's going to put the guard round the hospital, and everything will get back to normal.

The final numbers of those massacred at the Alexandra Hospital has never been fully established, but after the war, the British war crimes investigator said that as many as 100 medical staff and 100 wounded patients were killed outside the hospital. No estimate could be given for medical staff and patients killed inside the buildings. The Geneva Convention, which the Japanese had signed but never ratified, clearly states: 'It is illegal for soldiers to attack enemy troops displaying a flag of truce or a Red Cross hospital flag, thus avoiding needless casualties.'

The Japanese rode roughshod over the convention at the Alexandra Military Hospital in Singapore in February 1942.

Chapter 8
The Bataan Death March
April 1942

When the Japanese invaded the northern Philippine island of Luzon on 22 December 1941, they boasted that they would crush all resistance within forty-five days. The American and Filipino troops, commanded by Major General Edward P. King, retreated into the Bataan Peninsula at the northern tip of the island, where they held out for over three months, until on 9 April he had no choice but to surrender. After three months of combat, King's troops were exhausted, low on ammunition and food, with many suffering from malaria, dysentery and other diseases.

The following day, as dawn broke, the captured prisoners were gathered on an airfield near the village of Lucanin, south Lamao in Bataan province. They were stripped of their personal effects, and for some reason, any of them found to be in possession of Japanese money were immediately beheaded.

Worse was to come for the prisoners. General Homma, the officer in charge of the invading troops, informed Major General King that his men, including Filipinos, were to march from Bataan to the railhead of San Fernando, a distance of about 65 miles, and then on to Camp O'Donnell, a further 20 miles. Despite King's protests, the prisoners were soon to embark on a tragic six-day march along the Bataan Peninsula.

On 9 April 1942, the prisoners were split into groups of 100, setting off at intervals along a main road that led north towards their first camp. Most of the men were in a bad state due to the lack of supplies during their rearguard action, and some were so ill that they could hardly put one foot in front of the other. The heat and dust were intense as they staggered along. Sympathy from the Japanese guards was in short supply, and anyone who fell behind was simply shot, bayoneted, or beheaded, their bodies left lying by the roadside in full view of the following groups. When the guards stopped for food and drink, the men were made to sit in the sun without any cover, many simply dying in the intense heat.

Six Filipino soldiers who attempted escape were shot as they tried to run away, the guards draping their bodies over a wire fence to deter any others from the later groups from trying to escape. The Japanese justified this by referring to a domestic law they passed back in 1915, which called for the death penalty for prisoners who attempted to escape.

One American soldier called Lester Tenney talked about his experiences on the march after the war:

> If you fell out of line, you were dead. Well, this fellow fell out of line, and the Japanese officer came over, started talking to him and hollering, I'm telling him to get up and go and he didn't do it. And the Japanese officer just picked up his samurai sword… and went like this and hit the fellow on the back of the neck and went right straight through it and the head fell off and that's the part that's horrible and will live with you forever. Never forget it. You never forget seeing the head on the floor with his arms still moving his legs still moving but the head is off, never forget it no never.

One man who escaped from the march, American fighter pilot Captain Dyess, gave evidence when he got back to the US:

> The Japs seated us on the scorching ground, exposed to the full glare of the sun. Many of the Americans and Filipinos had no covering to protect their heads. I was beside a small bush, but it cast no shade because the sun was almost directly above us. Many of the men around me were ill. When I thought I could stand the penetrating heat no longer, I was determined to have a sip of the tepid water in my canteen. I had no more than unscrewed the top when the aluminium flask was snatched from my hands. The Jap who had crept up behind me poured the water into a horse's nosebag, then threw down the canteen. He walked on among the prisoners, taking away their water and pouring it into the bag. When he had enough, he gave it to his horse.

Captain Dyess suffered numerous beatings during the march but was making a mental catalogue of the treatment handed out to the prisoners – being beheaded, buried alive, run over by tanks, and used for bayonet practice. He was determined to report the atrocities to the outside world. A native of the tiny Texas town of Albany, Dyess became something of a living legend among the prisoners, who became known as 'The Battling Bastards of Bataan'. 'He was intelligent, magnetic, and fearless,' said one of his fellow escapees.

As the men marched along, many of the Filipinos living along the route offered them as much food and water as they could, despite the risks to themselves. A 10-year-old Filipino boy called Santiago Morales helped his uncle give out food to the soldiers as they passed their village:

> When the Japanese saw my uncle trying to help an American, they stabbed him in the armpit and the bayonet came out the other side. I was in shock. I couldn't speak because I knew that if I called for help the Japanese would kill me too. So, I kept silent, and my uncle died from his wound. The Japanese then shot the American and he died with my uncle on the same spot.

Lester Tenney again spoke about the atrocities carried out during the march:

> The Japanese called four men out of line and had them dig a ditch. When they dug the ditch, they told them to bury this man, one of the fellows said I can't bury him, he's still alive, so the Japanese shot this one man, called four more men out and said now dig this ditch. You don't want to bury your friend, you don't want to bury a live person, but you know that if you say no, you're going to be buried.

One of the American officers who survived, a Colonel Guy H. Stubbs, recalls many horrific incidents he saw on the march:

> Men were shot and bayoneted when they were too tired to walk. I saw five Japanese guards start to bury five Filipino soldiers in uniform alive after throwing them in a latrine and a Filipino being made to eat his own faeces. I saw a Filipino spread-eagled staked on the ground and was sure that the Filipino's hip joints were dislocated.

Stubbs stated that the prisoners did not offer any resistance or provoke their guards in any manner whatsoever. 'They were simply so weak that they could not keep up on the terribly long march. Most of them knew what was waiting for them if they fell, and they continued until they fell unconscious.'

Colonel Stubbs managed to survive not only the Bataan Death March, but four Japanese hell ships and twelve prison camps in the Philippines and Japan.

At the railhead at San Fernando, the prisoners were crammed into small railway wagons. Conditions were stifling and there was little air in the wagons; whilst the distance was only 35 miles, many men died standing up during the journey.

The first group of Filipino and American prisoners arrived at Camp O'Donnell on 11 April and the last on 4 June 1942. When they arrived, they discovered that conditions there were bad. Dyess again recalls:

> We were put in a barbed wire compound and seated in rows for a continuation of the sun treatment. Conditions here were the worst yet. The prison pen was jammed with sick, dying, and dead American and Filipino soldiers. They were sprawled amid the filth and maggots that covered the ground. Practically all had dysentery. Malaria and dengue fever appeared to be running unchecked. There were symptoms of other tropical diseases I didn't even recognize. Jap guards had shoved the worst cases beneath the rotted flooring of some dilapidated building. Many of these prisoners already had died. The others looked as though they couldn't survive until morning.
>
> There obviously had been no burials for many hours. After sunset Jap soldiers entered and inspected our rows. Then the gate was opened again, and kitchen corpsmen entered with cans of rice. We held our mess kits and again passed lids to those who had none. Our spirits rose. We watched as the Japs ladled out generous helpings to the men nearest the gate. Then, without explanation, the cans were dragged away, and the gate was closed. It was a repetition of the ghastly farce at Balanga. The fraud was much crueller this time because our need was vastly greater. In our bewildered state it took some time for the truth to sink in. When it did, we were too discouraged even to swear.

Over 9,000 American prisoners managed to survive the Bataan Death March, with more than 600 dying or being killed on the way. Filipino prisoners, numbering around 45,000, also arrived at the camp after completing the march, some 5,000 losing their lives.

From September 1942 to January 1943, the Japanese released the Filipino prisoners held in the camp on the understanding that they swore an oath not to become guerrillas, with the mayors of their hometowns made responsible for their conduct.

After the Filipinos had been released, the Japanese moved the American prisoners to Davao Penal Colony on the island of Mindanao. Three US officers tried to escape but were quickly recaptured; they were stripped, had their hands tied behind their backs and were hauled up with ropes. After two days in the hot sun, they were then taken down and shot. This did not deter Captain Dyess, who managed to escape along with nine others, assisted by two Filipinos, on 4 April 1943. This was the only large-scale prison break of Allied prisoners in the Pacific War. For weeks, the ten men managed to avoid Japanese search parties, trekking along jungle trails, over rugged mountains and paddling through swamps before eventually reaching Mindanao's northern coast. There they managed to join organised guerrilla units resisting the Japanese occupation.

Dyess and two others were evacuated from the island on the submarine USS *Trout* on 2 July 1943 and taken to Brisbane, Australia, where there they were able to tell the story of the Bataan Death March. When they eventually got back to the United States later that year, they became prisoners again in a different way. The US government were concerned that if the public were to find out about the treatment of their soldiers by the Japanese, a storm of bitterness might arise, and President Franklin D. Roosevelt forbade the men to tell their stories. This is the memo he sent at the time:

> September 9, 1943 MEMORANDUM FOR: The Secretary of War. The Secretary of the Navy. Subject: Japanese Atrocities – Reports of by Escaped Prisoners.
>
> 1. The publication of Japanese atrocities at this time might complicate the present and future missions of the GRIPSHOLM and increase the mistreatment of prisoners now in Japanese hands. I request, therefore, that you take effective measures to prevent the publication or circulation of any stories emanating from escaped prisoners until I have authorized a release.
> 2. It might be well for the Joint Chiefs of Staff to make recommendation as to the moment when I should inform the country of the mistreatment of our nationals.
>
> Signed F.D. Roosevelt

The story told by Dyess and his companions of the atrocities they had witnessed, was withheld for months by the US government in the fear that its publication would result in death to thousands of American prisoners still in Japanese hands.

It wasn't until Dyess died in an aircraft accident on 22 December 1943 that the government finally released his story. It was timed to harness the full fury of America's anger to aid the war effort by coinciding with the 'Fourth War Loan Drive', and was promoted as 'The Greatest Story of the War in the Pacific' and 'The biggest bombshell since Pearl Harbor'. It galvanised the American public into greater war efforts.

In the meantime, thousands of prisoners of war were still being ill-treated and murdered by the Japanese military across South East Asia.

Chapter 9
The Thai–Burma Railway
May 1942–August 1945

A mere two months after their attack on the US naval base at Pearl Harbor and their invasion of Malaya, the British colony of Singapore fell to the Japanese on 15 February 1942. The 'impregnable fortress', as it had been called, was now firmly in Japanese hands; around 130,000 Allied soldiers, including my own father, were now prisoners of war.

The following day, a deathly quiet hung over Singapore. Black smoke from the oil installation drifted overhead. The sight of the Rising Sun flags flying all over the city was demoralising for the defeated troops. Wrecked houses and burnt-out buildings lined the streets, dead bodies lay everywhere. Shops and cafés were boarded up. Japanese soldiers drove around wildly in stolen cars, grinning at the demoralised troops; some even demanded watches from the war-weary Allied soldiers. All watches and clocks in Singapore had to be put forward by one and a half hours to tie in with Tokyo time, and the island was renamed Syonan. Singapore was now hell on earth. The smell of defeat and utter desolation was everywhere.

The Japanese ordered the Allied commanders to move all their troops and equipment to Changi in the north-east corner of the island and for the next couple of months, Changi was a haven of peace for the exhausted troops after the previous few weeks of intense fighting.

The Japanese were totally unprepared for the number of prisoners on their hands and the men were initially left to look after themselves. My father said:

> In many ways, it didn't feel like a prison camp at all as we could move around freely within the perimeter. Our officers ran the camp in an organised military way and tried to make our lives as comfortable as possible during the early days of captivity.

With the British colonies of Burma and India now in their sights, rumours began circulating around Changi from early April 1942 that the Japanese were planning to send prisoners up into Thailand to help build a railway. Radios had been banned after the surrender, but with several clandestine sets operating, the men were aware that the Japanese had by now taken Rangoon, the capital of Burma, and were pushing northwards towards India. With such a swift advance, they were looking at other ways of resupplying their troops on the Burma front rather than by the dangerous sea journey up to Rangoon via the Straits of Malacca. With the Americans now in the war, their navy was posing a huge threat to Japanese shipping in the seas around Singapore.

The only safe and logical route for the Japanese to supply their Burma front line was overland from Bangkok in Thailand to Rangoon in Burma. The road network between the two cities was poor, with the only existing rail link a 40-mile stretch of track running from Bangkok to a small town called Ban Pong.

A decision was taken by the Japanese high command back in Tokyo that a railway link would be built between Nong Pladuk and the Burmese town of Thanbyuzayat, some 250 miles to the north-west. Such a link had been considered by the British many years earlier but was deemed just about impossible due to the difficulty of the terrain, with low-lying plains to the south, mountains up to 5,000 feet high and miles of dense tropical jungle. However, with all of Malaya in their hands and a puppet Thai government under their control, the Japanese decided to push ahead with this project regardless of the difficulties. They now had 130,000 'willing' and 'disposable' labourers to use however they liked.

Plans were quickly drawn up, with work scheduled to commence in June 1942 and a scheduled completion date of October 1943 – an incredibly ambitious feat. The start date was brought forward to May after the Japanese navy had been defeated at the Battle of Midway, weakening their ability to defend cargo ships taking supplies and ammunition from Singapore.

Groups of Allied prisoners of war began to leave Changi from April 1942 on a regular basis for Thailand as the Japanese started to build this 'impossible' railway. When it was first announced to the men in Changi that they were to be transported up into Thailand to work on the construction of the railway, many were excited about the prospect. The Japanese, through their interpreters, had painted a rosy picture of excellent living and working conditions in Thailand, with plentiful supplies of food and excellent medical facilities in a place where they would be well cared for. They said:

> The climate of the new location would be similar to that of Singapore, the men would be distributed around seven camps, all would be in pleasant and healthy surroundings, sufficient medical personnel to staff a 300 bed hospital could be sent, as many blankets and mosquito nets as possible were to be taken, a band could accompany each group of 1,000 men, canteens would be established within three weeks of arrival, no restriction would be placed on the amount of personal gear taken, tools and cooking gear were to be taken and transport would be available to take heavy goods and there would be no long marches.

Many of the prisoners believed these false promises and were happy to get away from the boring, crowded Changi camp.

The first group of prisoners to leave Changi for the railway, around 3,000 Australians, left Singapore in April 1942, bound by sea for Rangoon in Burma. During the following eighteen months, some 63,000 Allied prisoners of war were transported up into Thailand and Burma. My own father left Changi for the railway on 25 October 1942 and spent the next three years of his life toiling under a brutal and sadistic regime.

One of the world's leading experts on the Thai–Burma Railway, Rod Beattie, MBE, highlights the problems of its construction. He writes in his book *The Death Railway: A Brief History of the Thailand–Burma Railway*:

> During the planning of this railway link the Japanese engineers considered the many problems facing them, difficult terrain, climatic and health conditions, logistics, and the large amount of work involved. They made many decisions based on their appreciation of these problems. One important factor considered was the use of heavy construction machinery and this was rejected on the grounds of the almost impossible logistics of transporting, using, and maintaining such equipment. Therefore, their calculations were based on the principle that the work would be done by human labour.

The trains that transported the men 1,100 miles up into Thailand were made up of a series of metal cattle trucks around 20 feet long, 7 feet wide and 8 feet in height. There was only one entrance to each truck by a central sliding door about 6 feet wide. Thirty men, along with their kit, were crammed into each truck, leaving each man about 5 square feet. The only way they could make themselves comfortable was by sitting on top of their kit, and lying down was almost impossible. The trains only stopped when fuel and water were needed, giving the men an opportunity to relieve themselves on the nearest piece of ground. Water bottles could be filled from the water towers along the route. The only food they had to eat were the cooked rice balls given to them at Singapore station.

According to my father, the journey into Thailand was a nightmare:

> At Kuala Lumpur we stopped for an hour or so and were given a meal of weak stew and rice and very little water and I dreaded getting back into that steel box. The main problem was not food, but water and I was constantly thirsty.

After crossing into Thailand, the trains eventually arrived at Ban Pong station after a journey of 1,100 miles in forty hours on a train that was described by the men as simply hell on earth. Recalling his journey from Singapore, John Wyatt, a colleague of my father, who travelled up in June 1943, said:

> Dysentery cases weren't allowed off often enough, there was excrement everywhere and men simply wallowed in their own and other people's shit and piss for four days and nights. It was baking hot during the day and bitterly cold by night and dysentery had by now got a grip on many of the men.

The huts at Ban Pong were built of bamboo, with attap roofs, where the men would bed down for the night on flattened bamboo slats. The floors were often just a sea of mud and maggots or simply hard-baked earth, depending on the season. Cockroaches, ants and spiders crawled out from the cesspits that were used as latrines. Large bluebottles hummed and buzzed everywhere – a fertile breeding ground for diseases of all kinds.

Camps were built along the proposed route of the railway at regular intervals, with the distance between them varying depending on the difficulty of the work. On the flat plains, the camps were about 4 miles apart whilst in the mountains they were much closer together, and in many cases were built along the riverbank to allow supplies to be delivered by barges.

When the monsoon arrived in November 1942, progress on the railway slowed and conditions became even worse. During that time, many died from overwork, disease and malnutrition. In April 1943, with the construction well behind schedule, the Japanese called for greater effort from the malnourished prisoners, already slaving in terrible conditions. The 'speedo' phase was instigated to try to ensure that the railway was finished on schedule by the target date of October. Overnight working was introduced, with the prisoners having to work two eight-hour shifts in a day. Sick men were dragged out of their beds, regardless of how ill they were, and many died during this speedo period. The real 'atrocity' of the railway now began to unfold.

At the end of April 1943, a party of around 7,000 men, known as F Force, arrived at Ban Pong from Singapore, a group that was to suffer more than any other on the railway. Their destination was the Burmese border, around 200 miles to the north. In this group was a young Royal Army Medical Corps doctor called Frank Pantridge. (See end of chapter.)

When F Force arrived at Ban Pong, the railway had been completed as far as Wang Yai and there was no reason why they should not have been transported by train to there, but they were not. They were made to walk the 200 miles to their camps up near the Burmese border, a trek that took seventeen days. Many of the men were not able to complete the march, dropping out at camps along the way, whilst others died and were left behind on the jungle tracks.

The most important facility in each camp on the Thai–Burma Railway was the latrine. It was necessary to site them close to the huts so that the men who were suffering from dysentery and other digestive illnesses could reach them easily. This was often counterproductive, however, as they attracted flies, bluebottles and other insects close to the living quarters. The latrines were usually simply a trench with bamboo poles laid across for the men to squat on. As most of the camps were situated near the river, the water levels would rise during the monsoon season, polluting the whole area.

Cholera spread like wildfire through the camps on the railway. John Wyatt told me:

> Someone in the bed next to you would be alive when you went out on a 'speedo' work detail in the morning and by the end of the shift, his bed space would be empty. At this camp, my comrades were dying at the rate of ten a day and the Japanese instructed us to dig deep pits to bury the bodies. One morning Doctor Roy asked for four volunteers to bury some bodies, so my mate and I, along with two others, put up

> our hands. We walked about half a mile to a deep pit where five bodies lay wrapped in rice sacks with ropes tied around their ankles, stomachs, and necks. We hurriedly lowered the first four bodies on ropes into the pit and as we began to lower the last one in, the sacking came off his face. As I lowered him into the stinking pit, a tear fell from my eye. A bit later, the Japanese decided that it was better to burn the bodies rather than bury them and I was relieved not to be detailed any more to that horrible task. We could clearly see the flames and smoke from the fires at night and smell the burning flesh.

Although extremely difficult and nigh-on impossible from such a remote area, escape was still on many men's minds. In January 1943, three men attempted to escape during a march from Ban Pong to Chungkai but were quickly recaptured and executed. Bugler Arthur Lane of the Manchester Regiment, whom I had the good fortune to befriend before he passed away in 2018, told me that he played the Last Post at the execution of these unfortunate men. Lane recalls:

> They managed to slip away from the main body of men with the intention of stealing a boat or swimming across the river. They were betrayed by Thai villagers and handed over to the Japanese for the bounty money on offer. They were duly tried and sentenced to death. The news would have been catastrophic to those who were working on the railway, so the matter was kept secret. In agreement, I kept the knowledge to myself at the time, only recording their names on the list of funerals I attended to sound the Last Post. It was intended that the four men should be executed in front of the other prisoners as an example, but due to pressure from senior officers headed by Lieutenant Colonel Toosey at Kanchanaburi, their execution took place on 4 February 1943 in semi-secrecy just behind what was later to become Chungkai Cemetery. The four are buried in Kanchanaburi Cemetery.

The Thai–Burma Railway was finally completed on 17 October 1943, when track-laying parties from both the Thailand end and the Burmese end met at Konkoita. Over 150 million cubic feet of earth had been moved and 9 miles of bridges had been built by the prisoners in sixteen months.

A Japanese general hammered a golden spike into the track, at least that is what the men were told at the time, but the spike was made of copper, not gold. (The original spike is exhibited in the Death Railway Museum in Kanchanaburi, a museum that is well worth a visit if you are in the area.)

As a C56 locomotive was driven ceremoniously along the section of track, the prisoners were lined up to witness the achievement. In honour of their efforts, they were given 2 ounces of soap, ten Thai cigarettes and fruit to celebrate, items that had probably come from Red Cross parcels that had been withheld from them. Wreaths were laid in honour of the Allied prisoners who died on the railway and a Japanese officer made a speech to the men:

> Thank you very much for realising the importance of the railway to Nippon. We are sorry some of your friends have died but it is the duty of the soldier to die when necessary. Soon you will be going back to Kanchanaburi and Nong Pladuk. Continue to be good soldiers. Take care of your health so that when peace comes you may return to your own country, to your dear wives and children and to all your dear friends.

One can only imagine what was going through the minds of the prisoners of war who lined up to witness this speech.

When the railway was completed, many of the surviving prisoners, who were by now in a terrible physical and mental state, were evacuated by train down to Kanchanaburi and Nong Pladuk. The remnants of F Force were put on trains to Singapore, leaving behind the bodies some 1,060 Australian and 2,036 British soldiers. Many were sick, starved walking skeletons. F Force's overall death rate was 45 per cent compared to the average of 20 per cent on the railway.

Now fully operational, trains loaded with troops and supplies creaked and groaned their way north towards Burma, along the railway tracks that had seen so many deaths. It is said that there was a death for every sleeper. The Japanese train crews would not have been aware of the cost in human lives as they picked their way over the skeletons of the dead along the line. They would not see the ghosts of the hundreds of men that crept silently in and out of the jungle and across the line. The Japanese had achieved their objective in building a railway by a display of callous cruelty and complete disregard for human life.

During the three and a half years when my father and the other hundreds of prisoners of war were in captivity, Red Cross parcels were sent from Britain, Australia and the US via Switzerland. Most of these parcels were never distributed to the men in captivity and were retained by the Japanese. In some of the camps, the men were aware that Red Cross parcels were stored, but if they attempted to get to them and were caught, they would be beaten and tortured.

As 1944 drew to a close, the railway came under attack from Allied aircraft flying from Burma. It was an obvious target at that time as its destruction would limit the Japanese effort to resupply their troops on the Burmese front. Their storage base at Nong Pladuk also became a prime target, along with the many bridges on the railway. By early 1945, many parts of it had been blown to pieces.

Many of the men, including my father, were unable to forgive or forget their treatment at the hands of the Japanese on the Thai–Burma Railway. To the day he died, my father would never buy anything Japanese. He died at the age of 73 of cancer of the oesophagus and his last words to me were: 'The Japanese did this to me.' Of course, we have no way of knowing if this was due to his treatment on the Thai–Burma Railway. He was not alone in his hatred of the Japanese. Arthur Lane was never able to escape his haunting experiences, and his hate for the Japanese burned like a fire in his heart and mind until the day he died. A bugler with the Manchester Regiment, Lane played the Last Post over the graves of hundreds of men who died of disease and starvation on the railway during his three years as a prisoner of war. His bitterness knew no bounds.

By early 1942, Japan had over 200 million conquered people under its control. Official Japanese policy towards these people was *hakko ichiu*, 'all the world under a single roof'.

* Frank Pantridge, F Force: On returning to his native Belfast in October 1945, despite still being very weak from weight loss, vitamin deficiency and hypertension, Pantridge's first priority was to resume his medical career. After his experiences while enduring beriberi in the prisoner of war camps, he began to specialise in diseases of the heart. He was aware that most sudden deaths from heart problems occurred because of ventricular fibrillation, a disturbance in the heart rhythm, and he was convinced that if an electric

shock could be applied to the chest as soon as possible after a cardiac arrest, the patient might be saved. He began to think of ways to take the large and bulky defibrillators that were available in the hospitals out to patients and in 1965, he produced the world's first portable defibrillator. One of his defibrillators saved American President Lyndon B. Johnson in 1972. Johnson said, 'I owe my life to the invention of this former Japanese prisoner of war.'

Pantridge nearly died several times during his captivity and is famously quoted as saying, 'I will not leave my bloody bones in Burma.'

Chapter 10

Atrocities at Sea

December 1941–March 1945

During the Second World War, the Allied navies did their best to help a beaten enemy wherever possible, and on many occasions, Allied seamen risked their own lives to help others who were previously their enemy. German U-boat commanders often surfaced to try to help any survivors from ships they had sunk or damaged, usually giving the survivors some food, cigarettes, or an indication of where the nearest land was. They knew that the common enemy to all sailors was the sea. The Japanese Imperial Navy, despite its officers being trained by the British Navy, saw things differently, as you are to discover later in this chapter.

On 10 December 1941, three days after the attack on Pearl Harbor, the Panamanian flagship *Donerail*, carrying a cargo of sugar and pineapples, was sunk just south of Hawaii by the Japanese submarine *I-10*, commanded by Lieutenant Commander Kayahara. The *Donerail*'s crew of forty-three managed to get away in lifeboats, but they were machine-gunned by the *I-10*, with only sixteen crew members surviving. This is the earliest recorded atrocity by the Japanese at sea during the war.

Twenty-two days later, on New Year's Day 1942, the Dutch ship *Langkoeas* left Surabaya on Java bound for Haifa in Israel with a full cargo of sugar. The ship was commanded by Captain Jan Kreumer and had a crew of ninety-three. On the evening of the following day, the *Langkoeas* was attacked by the Japanese submarine *I-58*, commanded by Lieutenant Commander Soshichi Kitamura, one of its torpedoes scoring a direct hit. Chaos broke out on board the *Langkoeas*, with the Chinese and Javanese crew running around in panic. Realising the ship was doomed, Captain Kreumer ordered 'abandon ship'. One of its four lifeboats had been destroyed, whilst another was dropped overboard as the crew tried to launch it, but most of the surviving crew managed to cram into the two remaining lifeboats. By now, the Japanese submarine had surfaced and was bearing down on the survivors, who hoped that they would be rescued – but this was not to be. Kitamura ordered his crew to open fire on the helpless men, and within minutes, the lifeboats had been sunk, leaving seventy-five lifeless bodies floating in the sea. One of the crewmembers who managed to survive, Jan de Mul, saw the submarine coming towards him and grabbed hold of one of its hydroplanes. He was dragged through the water for several minutes before the vessel slowed to a halt, when Japanese hands reached down and dragged him onto the deck. Realising his predicament, he tried to escape and jump overboard, but one of the crewmembers slashed his leg with a sword. De Mul was then taken into the conning tower, where he was interrogated by Kitamura under threat of death if he didn't give him the information he requested. Once Kitamura had finished questioning him, the crew punched and kicked him before throwing him back into the sea. Fortunately, still wearing his life jacket, he was able to swim clear of the submarine as it submerged. De Mul floated in the oily sea for several hours before finding the *Langkoeas*' 12-footer work boat and climbed aboard. Later he saw one of the Chinese crew drifting by and managed to rescue him, along with a Javanese. The three men spent some four or five days under the intense sun, without any drinking water or food, before finally washing up ashore on Bawean, an island in the Java Sea. They were later picked up by a Dutch Catalina flying boat and brought to Soerabaja (Surabaya), where they told their story. Out of a crew of 93, only 2 others survived along with De Mul, 12 dying in the engine room when the torpedo hit, whilst 75 died in the machine-gunning. Lieutenant Commander Kitamura was never brought to trial for this atrocity.

After the Japanese had taken Malaya and Singapore, they set their eyes on Australia, mainly with the intention of cutting off supplies and denying the country as a base to either America or Britain. On 19 February 1942, a Japanese fleet of aircraft carriers attacked Darwin, Australia's only port in the north. With little in the way of air defences, the Japanese aircraft were able to bomb the ships in the harbour and reduce the town to smoking ruins. Not content with damaging the ships and the town, the pilots proceeded to machine-gun survivors in lifeboats or who were struggling in the water. Eight ships were sunk, with nine others severely damaged. One hundred and seventy seamen were dead. One man, Second Officer Pierre Payne, who was serving on board the tanker *British Motorist* at the time, tells of the attack:

> When we were attacked, our Indian crew were panicking and eventually we had to abandon ship. The chief officer stayed on the ship to look after the captain who had a leg blown off. I managed to get a boat away and decided to make for the shore rather than the jetty, which was fortunate. A ship alongside the jetty laden with depth charges blew up. But that was war. What we did not like was when they turned their attention to the Australian hospital ship which was clearly marked – painted with red crosses. They bombed and machine-gunned her. That was not war. That was sheer murder.

On 27 February 1942, a Dutch oil tanker, the *Augustina*, under the command of Captain A.J. Moerman, left Tanjung Priok on Java's north-west coast, heading for Australia. Two days later, 300 miles south of Christmas Island, the Japanese destroyer *Harukaze*, caught up with her. Realising that the ship was doomed and would be sunk, the captain scuttled her and abandoned ship, the crew getting away in two lifeboats. The boats were taken in tow by the destroyer, with the captain and first engineer taken on board for questioning, before being thrown back into a lifeboat. The boats were then cut loose and the men ordered to row away, thinking they were now safe, but the captain of the *Harukaze* had other ideas and opened up on the defenceless men with machine guns. Only one man survived to tell the tale.

During the early months of 1942, and with many of their young men away fighting the war, the Japanese government decided that they would start to ship Allied prisoners of war to Japan to make up a shortage of labour in their factories and mines. Whilst prisoners of war were a readily available and disposable supply of cheap labour, they were scattered all over South East Asia, and transporting them to the home islands and elsewhere was to prove a difficult task. Between 15 May 1942 and 31 January 1945, around 130 Japanese registered ships left from various ports, shipping prisoners of war to locations where labour was needed. These ships were to become known as 'hell ships'.

On 23 December 1941, Wake Island, a coral atoll in the western Pacific Ocean in the north-eastern area of the Micronesia subregion, fell to the Japanese, with around 1,600 American servicemen and civilians taken prisoner. On 12 January 1942, most of them were taken down to the docks, where they were herded into the hold of the *Nitta Maru*, a former luxury liner, bound for Shanghai via Yokohama. Before boarding, they were sprayed with what one man described as 'smelly insecticide' and then packed in like sardines and ordered to sit still. Anyone who moved was beaten by the Japanese guards. One American corporal said that he wasn't allowed to stand up for the full eleven days of the journey. Water was in short supply and some men resorted to licking condensation off the metal sides of the ship. They were fed a diet of thin rice soup supplemented by some small pieces of pickled radish, fish heads or guts.

As the *Nitta Maru* headed north-west in the North Pacific towards Yokohama during a bitter Japanese winter, the prisoners were freezing. Although they had been issued with thin blankets before leaving, they were not thick enough to ward off the bitter cold, and this was made worse by the lack of food and water.

When the ship docked in Yokohama six days later, on 18 January, the guards opened the hatches and threw snowballs at the prisoners to celebrate their arrival onto Japanese soil. They were kept locked in the hold for two more days before the *Nitta* set off again for Shanghai. During this leg of the journey, their treatment got worse. Five airmen were brought up from the holds to be tried in a kangaroo court by the guards' commander, who stood on a box and said:

> You have killed many Japanese soldiers in battle. For what you have done you are now going to be killed for revenge. You are here as representatives of your American soldiers, and you will be killed. You can now pray to be happy in the next world in heaven.

The five airmen were blindfolded and forced to kneel with their heads bent forward, before the guards brought their swords down on their necks as the Japanese clapped their hands. After the war, one of the Japanese sailors said:

> The sword was brought down on the neck of the first victim making a swishing noise as it cut the air. As the blade hit and pierced the flesh it gave a resounding noise like a wet towel being flipped or shaken out. The body of the first victim lay quietly, half across a mat and half onto the wooden deck.

After the men had been slaughtered, some of the guards tried to cut the corpses in two with a single sword stroke, before throwing the mangled bodies into the ocean.

When the *Nitta Maru* docked in Shanghai on 23 January, after an eleven-day voyage from hell, the prisoners were marched to a camp 5 miles away, an old unheated wooden barracks surrounded by an electric fence, where they remained until the end of the war.

Five months later, on 22 June 1942, the *Montevideo Maru* left Rabaul in Papua New Guinea bound for Samah, on the island of Hainan in the South China Sea. Papua New Guinea had fallen to the Japanese at the end of January, when over 1,000 Australians of the 2/22 battalion, known as Lark Force, were taken prisoner. Along with around 200 civilians, they were loaded onto the ship, and it set off without an escort. Conditions on board were bad for the men, with very little food or water given. The *Montevideo Maru* could travel at 18 knots, fast enough to outrun most of the American submarines. As the prisoners languished in the heat of the holds, crammed together like animals, the ship sailed through the treacherous Red Channel, west of New Ireland and then on through the Philippine Sea.

On 30 June, ten days into the voyage, the American submarine *Sturgeon*, commanded by Lieutenant Commander William L. Wright, was patrolling about 60 miles north-west of Luzon when it spotted the *Montevideo*. Just after midnight, the submarine unleashed four torpedoes towards the ship and within twelve minutes, the *Montevideo* had sunk. The *Sturgeon* quickly steamed out of the area, unaware that it contained prisoners of war and of the carnage it had left behind.

As the ship went down, the Japanese launched the lifeboats, ignoring the prisoners who were still locked in the holds. Some of them managed to break out and jump into lifeboats that had been damaged but were still afloat, but many others were drowned in the holds.

None of the Australians survived the attack and subsequent sinking, either going down with the ship or dying of thirst and starvation in the lifeboats.

The relatives of the men, back in Australia, were not to find out about the fate of their loved ones until almost four years later. The *Montevideo Maru* was the first hell ship loaded with prisoners of war to be sunk by a US submarine, but it was not to be the last.

On 27 September 1942, another tragedy occurred when the *Lisbon Maru* left Hong Kong bound for Shanghai. Around 2,000 prisoners of war, led by Colonel Stewart of the Middlesex Regiment, and including men of the Royal Navy, the Royal Scots, the Middlesex Regiment and the Royal Artillery, were forced onto the ship. Also on board were some 778 Japanese troops returning home. The *Lisbon* was under the command of Captain Kyoda Shigeru and the prisoners under the command of an army officer called Wada Hideo, assisted by an interpreter called Niimori Genichiro.

The men were crammed down into cargo holds that had been fitted out with wooden platforms. Conditions in the holds were atrocious; cold damp and filthy, but surprisingly, the food was reasonable and there was plenty of drinking water.

The first four days at sea were uneventful, until the early morning of 1 October, when the American submarine *Grouper*, captained by Lieutenant Commander Rob McGregor, spotted the ship in the East China Sea just south of Shanghai. The *Grouper* fired three torpedoes at the *Lisbon*, which all missed, but the fourth one scored a direct hit. However, the *Lisbon* did not sink. By now, the water supply had run out and with the hatches battened down, there was little air supply for the prisoners. Colonel Stewart asked if the men could go on deck and was told by the ship's captain, Kyoda Shigeru: 'You bred like rats so you can stay like rats in a cage.'

Late in the afternoon, the Japanese destroyer *Kuri* came alongside and took off most of the Japanese soldiers, leaving the prisoners still locked in the holds. The *Lisbon Maru* then staggered along through the night, towed by the destroyer, with the men in the holds baling out furiously. Some of them were in such a bad way that they died during that awful night. Just before dawn, the tow rope broke; leaving the *Lisbon* to its fate, the Japanese navy's attempt to rescue it had failed and it was obvious to the men down in the holds that they were being left to die. A small group of Japanese soldiers on deck stood over the hatches armed with rifles to prevent anyone escaping. Realising their fate, many of the men began to sing, until the seawater stifled and choked their voices mid-note.

At around 0800 hrs, the ship lurched and began to sink. Colonel Stewart ordered the men to make a run for the hatches and try to break out, but as they emerged, the Japanese soldiers left on board to guard them opened fire. Hundreds of men who fought their way up the ladders onto the deck managed to overpower the guards and brutally kill them in revenge.

The Japanese sailors who were in the lifeboats kicked the survivors off as they tried to join them. As the men frantically tried to escape, a ladder broke, leaving them with no way out. The stronger swimmers who did make it into

Shirō Ishii, the head of Unit 731. When the war ended, Ishii went into hiding in Japan. General Douglas MacArthur exonerated Ishii and his senior doctors of war crimes, in exchange for handing over all his documents relating to the results of his experiments, one of which came to 12,000 pages.

Japanese troops bayoneting Chinese troops in Nanking, December 1937.

Chinese soldiers about to be executed by Japanese troops, Nanking.

Sketch of the Sook Ching Massacre, February 1942.

Plaque in the grounds of the Alexandra Hospital, Singapore, commemorating the massacre of February 1942.

Lieutenant Colonel Vivian Bullwinkel, the sole survivor of the Bangka Island Massacre, 12–14 February 1942, when the Japanese murdered twenty-one army nurses. Bullwinkle went on to become one of Australia's most distinguished women.

Artist's impression of the Bangka Island Massacre.

The Bataan Death March – captured soldiers carrying Japanese supplies.

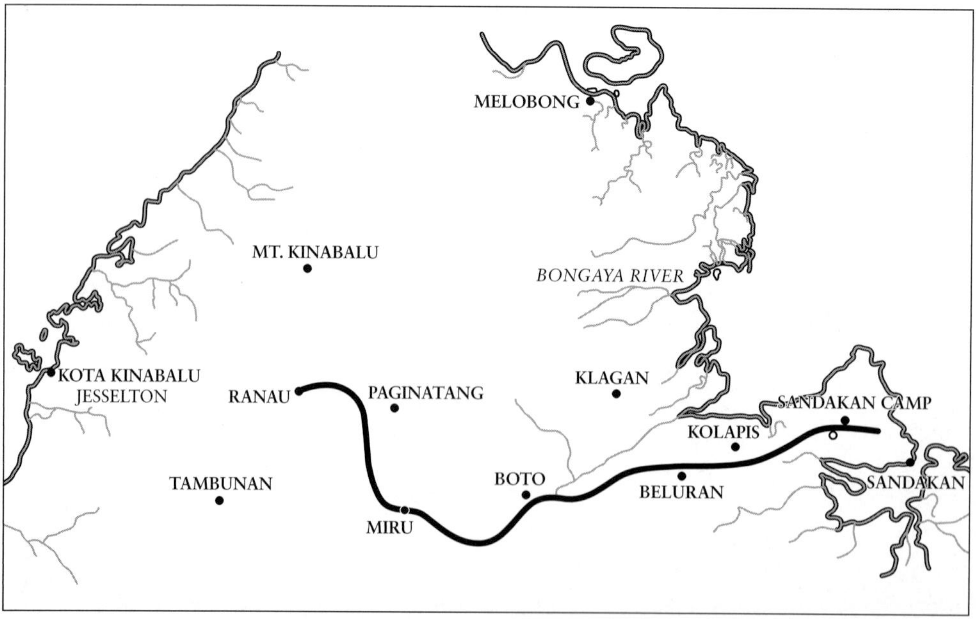

Map of the Sandakan death marches.

Japanese soldiers accused of atrocities during the Sandakan death marches.

Rock inscription carved by prisoners on a beach, Wake Island, 1943.

The pig baskets used to transport prisoners to their deaths in October 1942 on Java.

Len Siffleet (left), a member of the AIF Special Unit, being led away to be beheaded by the Japanese in New Guinea on 24 October 1943.

A suspected Japanese war criminal is identified by an Indian Army officer, at Rabaul, New Guinea.

Japanese prisoners in the dock during the first war crimes trial held in Rangoon, Burma. These men were charged with the murder of 637 civilians in the village of Kalagon, Burma.

General Tomoyuki Yamashita, the most notorious Japanese officer who was convicted of war crimes, in particular for the 'Rape of Manila' and the Alexandra Hospital Massacre. Yamashita was found guilty of failing to prevent the massacres and atrocities and was sentenced to be executed in February 1946.

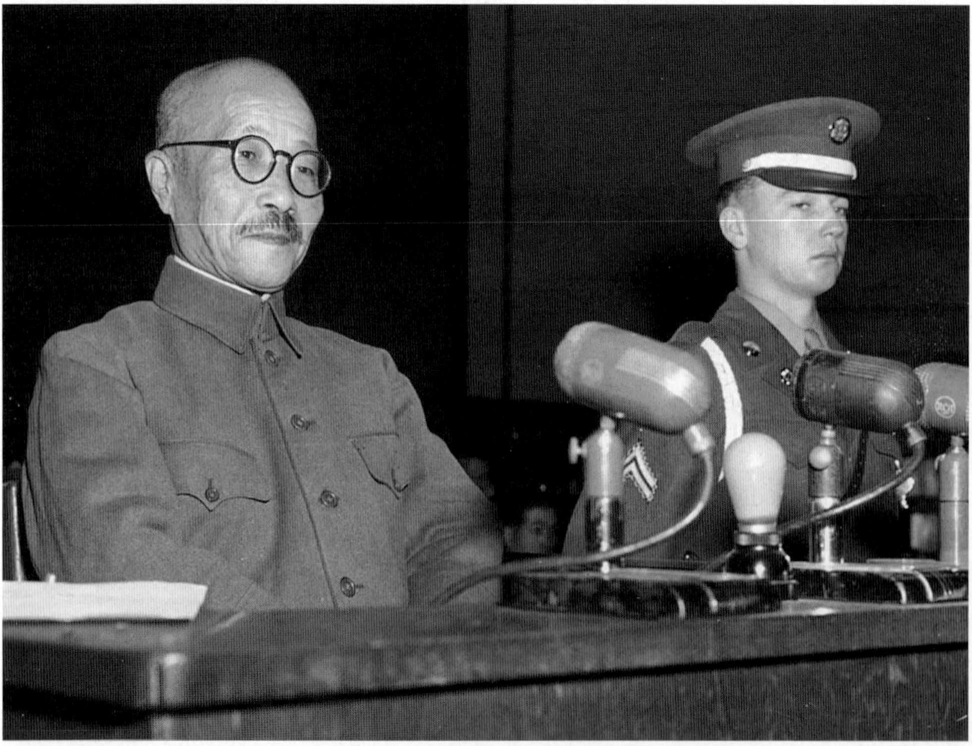

General Hideki Tōjō at his trial in Tokyo, 1947. He was found guilty and hanged.

the sea started swimming furiously towards nearby islands, and some were lucky enough to reach their sandy beaches. Some of the more unfortunate ones were washed onto the sharp rocks that surrounded some of the islands, whilst others swam towards the Japanese destroyer *Kuri*, hoping to be rescued. As they approached it, they were shot at, or bayoneted as they tried to climb aboard. Watching from a distance were some Chinese fishermen who lived on the islands who, initially thinking that the survivors were Japanese, turned a blind eye to proceedings, but on realising that they were in fact British, quickly launched boats into the area and started picking them up, collecting several hundred soldiers and tending to their wounds. These brave fishermen managed to pick up 384 men and take them back to land, where they fed and looked after them, despite the dangers if they were caught by the Japanese. These brave Chinese fishermen were rewarded for the risks that they took and were able to purchase a brand-new motorised fishing boat from the donations of the men who survived the rescue and imprisonment.

The men who had now survived and were on the island discussed possible plans for an escape, but these were soon dashed when a Japanese destroyer moored up nearby and a group of Japanese marines came ashore and recaptured them. They were then taken to a wharf on the Whangpoo River in Shanghai, where around thirty-six of the seriously ill were taken to hospital, where they received adequate treatment.

The fortunate survivors were then issued with a small amount of rice and given new clothing before being put on another ship, called the *Shinsei Maru*, bound for Japan. Five more men died on board the *Shinsei Maru*; the remaining men were moved on to spend the rest of the war in a prison camp at Kobe. At Kobe, 244 died as prisoners of war. Of the original 1,816 prisoners of war who boarded the *Lisbon Maru*, 1,091 had drowned, been killed or died in prison camps.

In early March 1943, the Japanese destroyer *Akikaze*, commanded by Lieutenant Commander Sabe Tsurukichi, docked at Wewak in New Guinea, before sailing on to a small island called Kairiru, also known as D'Urville Island. Tsurukichi's task was to round up some German missionaries who were suspected of using radio transmitters to report ship movements to the Americans. The missionaries were willing to risk their lives for the Allied cause and had helped some airmen who had been shot down.

At Kairiru, around forty people were taken on board, including several clergymen, along with some nuns and two children. The *Akikaze* then proceeded on to Manus Island, halfway between Kairiru and New Ireland, where thirty more civilians were picked up before heading on to Rabaul in Papua New Guinea.

As the ship ploughed along, Tsurukichi received a message from his fleet headquarters to dispose of his human cargo. Whilst reluctant to do this, but as it was an order, he had no option but to carry it out. No reason was given as to why they should be executed.

A wooden platform was built on the deck with a sheet hung up in front of it. The unfortunate civilian victims were then blindfolded and taken to the platform, where they were hung up by their wrists and shot, their bodies being then flung over the side. The two children on board were snatched from the arms of the nuns who were looking after them and thrown overboard. Afterwards, the Japanese officers cynically conducted a ceremony for the deceased.

On 5 May 1943, the *Thames Maru* left Singapore bound for the Palau islands, 400 miles to the east of the Philippines. On board were over 2,000 Indian, Indonesian, Malay and Chinese prisoners – the first time non-Europeans had been shipped overseas. Conditions on the ship were dreadful, with around 200 dying during a voyage that took just over three weeks. The surviving prisoners were put to work on Babelthuap Island breaking up coral, digging trenches and clearing land for the construction of an airfield. When the island was liberated in August 1945, 117 more had died.

On 12 May 1943, the Australian hospital ship *Centaur*, commanded by Captain George Murray, with 283 medical personnel on board, sailed from Sydney bound for Port Moresby to evacuate sick and injured soldiers. The ship was clearly marked with a red cross, leaving no doubt that she was a hospital ship.

On the morning of the 14th, the *Centaur* was 40 miles east of Brisbane, heading north towards the Torres Strait, when the Japanese submarine *I-177*, commanded by Lieutenant Commander H. Nakagawa, spotted it. There was no doubt that he knew it was a hospital ship, but nonetheless, he ordered torpedoes to be fired, one of which penetrated well below the waterline and hit a tank carrying fuel oil. Within minutes, the *Centaur* was ablaze and Captain Murray ordered 'abandon ship'. The vessel went down so quickly that the crew had no time to launch the lifeboats and were forced to jump into the sea, clinging on to any wreckage that was available.

For the next twenty-four hours, the survivors drifted in the Coral Sea. Sixty-three survivors made-up of twenty-nine of the *Centaur*'s crew and thirty-four medical personnel including one nurse, were eventually rescued by an American destroyer, the USS *Mugford*. Out of the hospital ship's total compliment of 360, those who were lost numbered 297 – including eleven nurses.

When news of the sinking got back to Australia, the government sent a message to the Japanese via diplomatic channels complaining bitterly about the sinking of an unarmed hospital ship:

> His majesty's government in the Commonwealth of Australia most emphatically protests to the Japanese government against this wanton attack in disregard not only of the Hague Convention and of International Law, but also of the principles of common humanity accepted by all civilised nations. The Commonwealth Government demands that those responsible for the attack should be punished immediately and demands assurance from the Japanese government that there will be no repetition by the Forces under the command of the Japanese government of such an incident in violation of International Law and practice. The Commonwealth Government reserves the right to claim full indemnification and redress for losses sustained.

Of course, this protest was never replied to, as the Japanese Navy were a law unto themselves at that time.

The *Taga Maru* left Manila in the Philippines bound for Moji, Japan, on 20 September 1943. On board were 850 American prisoners of war. During a voyage that lasted fifteen days, the prisoners got little food, water, or medical attention, with seventy men dying. Private Henry Stanley of the 27th Bomber Group of the US Air Force, who was on board, recalled the conditions:

> For a few days we could make it without too much food, but you cannot live without water. The only air in the hold came from one open hatch,

> and many men in the corners suffocated. A lot of the guys drank their own urine, they died like flies.

The highest death rate during 1943 came from the *Suez Maru*, a ship that left Ambon, part of the Maluku Islands of Indonesia, bound for Java on 25 November that year. On board were 546 British prisoners of war, twenty of whom were stretcher cases. The *Suez* was accompanied by the *Nichinan Maru* and a minesweeper under the command of Captain Kawano. The Japanese officer in charge of the prisoners, Lieutenant Iketani Masaji, asked his superior officer before leaving: 'If this ship is attacked by torpedoes from enemy submarines and sinks, what measures shall be taken? And what should be done if the escort ship hasn't the capacity to accommodate everybody?' His commander replied: 'You may shoot them.'

The following day, 26 November, the American submarine *Bonefish*, under the direction of Commander Tom Hogan, spotted the ships making heavy black smoke in the Java Sea and unleashed two torpedoes at the *Suez*. Within minutes, it had slipped below the waves, taking 300 prisoners with it and leaving the sea littered with debris. Only 246 managed to get out of the holds in time.

The Japanese minesweeper returned to pick up the Japanese survivors, leaving the prisoners who had escaped to their fate as they swam around frantically looking for anything to cling on to. The minesweeper then circled the distraught prisoners as they waved frantically, hoping to be taken on board. Lieutenant Iketani Masaji's orders were then carried out when suddenly its machine guns opened fire on the helpless men, who tried to hide behind any sort of wreckage they could find. Some of them who had managed to get on life rafts stood up with their arms aloft, inviting the bullets in a defiant gesture. Every single one of the 246 men was annihilated. When Captain Kawano was finally assured that every prisoner of war was dead, he rammed through the debris and the bodies before leaving the area heading for Java.

When the minesweeper arrived at Surabaya, Kawano falsified war records by stating:

> The enemy torpedoed the *Suez Maru*, and that, because of the need for strict security, all the prisoners were kept locked in the holds, so they all went down with the ship, and that, no survivors could be found despite rescue attempts. They were all killed by their own people.

On 8 December 1943, the British cargo steamer *Daisy Moller*, under the command of Captain Reginald Weeks, left Colombo heading across the Bay of Bengal for Chittagong. On board were a total crew of seventy-one, made-up of Indian and Chinese ratings along with six Royal Navy men manning the ship's ancient guns.

The first six days of the voyage were uneventful, until at around 0430 hrs on the 14th, the *Moller* was hit by a torpedo fired from the Japanese submarine *RO-110*, commanded by Kazuro Ebato. With the ship sinking rapidly and concerned about the ammunition it was carrying, Weeks ordered 'abandon ship'. The lifeboats were launched and the crew managed to scramble aboard minutes before the *Moller* slipped beneath the waves. Fortunately, all crewmembers managed to get into the lifeboats and away before it sank. Their luck was not to last, however, as the *R-110* surfaced close by and proceeded to ram through the lifeboats, splintering them and causing the men to jump overboard. To make matters worse, the submarine opened fire on them as they thrashed around in the water.

By dawn the next morning, the waters above the sunken *Daisy Moller* were red with the blood of the murdered seamen. Out of the crew of seventy-one, fifty-five bodies now floated in the sea. Sixteen men had managed to survive the carnage, eventually reaching the shore at Masulipatam.

Some justice was handed out as the *E-110* was sunk two months later, when Ebato and all his crew drowned.

On 19 February 1944, the British cargo ship SS *Ascot* left Columbo in Sri Lanka (now Ceylon) bound for Diego Suarez, Madagascar. By now, Japanese submarines were operating in the Indian Ocean and shortly after noon on 29 February, the ship was hit by torpedoes fired from the submarine *I-37*. The engine room was ripped apart and the *Ascot* began to sink rapidly. The crew were able to launch several lifeboats, with all but four of the fifty-six managing to get off the ship. Ten minutes later, the *I-37* surfaced about a quarter of a mile away and began to approach the lifeboats. The submarine's captain, Lieutenant Commander Nakagawa, ordered the *Ascot*'s captain, James Travis, to come aboard his vessel. After questioning him for a few minutes, his hands were slashed and he was pushed back into the water, from where he was picked up by a lifeboat. The submarine then opened fire on the survivors who had jumped into the sea, killing ten of them. One of only eight survivors, A.H. Taylor recalls vividly what happened that fateful evening:

> We could see a light calibre machine gun on the tower, and we knew that we were in for trouble. Some of us thought it time to go over the side and did so. The *I-37* machine-gunned the two boats and the raft as well as anyone in the water for a considerable period. The raft was very solidly constructed and, after the first few bursts, also covered with bodies, so those of us still alive tried to keep it between the submarine and ourselves. The trouble was that we were spinning it and it became hard work. Several people drifted away, possibly shot, but more probably exhausted. Nakagawa then turned his attention to the ship and shelled it setting her on fire though she remained afloat. We all tidied up by disposing of bodies and putting out tow lines. However, the *I-37* returned and shot us up with machine guns, rifles, and pistols for another long session. It used its screws to try to wash us off and to ram one or more of the boats, but after a couple of hours or so Nakagawa either thought he had killed us all or decided he had spent long enough and left. The ship sank after dark, and we were alone, the only survivors being Harry Fortune, who was eighteen, myself (still seventeen) the three A.B.s and two gunners. One A.B. was shot in the shoulder and one gunner in the thigh. The following day we found two thirds of a lifeboat with gunner Bill Hughson in it. The boat had been rammed but he had feigned dead and been left alone.

The survivors were picked up a short time later by a Dutch motor vessel called the *Straat Soenda* and landed at Aden six days later to tell the grim story of the sinking of the *Ascot*. Nakagawa was considered one of the most feared and hated submarine commanders during the Second World War, and in January 1947, he pleaded guilty for his wartime crimes before the International Military Tribunal in Tokyo. He was sentenced to eight years of hard labour; but only served six and was released on probation after the end of the Allied Occupation.

In the Indian Ocean on 18 March 1944, the Japanese submarine *I-165*, commanded by Lieutenant Shimizu, fired two torpedoes at the British merchant ship SS *Nancy Moller*. The *Moller* had left Durban, South Africa, two weeks earlier bound for Colombo, Ceylon, with a full cargo of coal. Both torpedoes hit the ship in quick succession on her port side and she sank in less than a minute, with some of the crew managing to get away on life rafts.

The submarine surfaced 50 yards away and drew alongside one of the life rafts, when the survivors were asked where the captain and chief engineer were. The men reported that the captain and chief engineer had gone down with the ship. The six men on the raft, including gunlayer Dennis Fryer, were then taken on board the submarine. Fryer was taken below, whilst the other five, two Chinese and three Indian sailors, were forced to kneel on the deck before being shot in the back and then kicked overboard. The Japanese sailors then proceeded to machine-gun any other survivors they saw clinging to debris in the vicinity before departing the area. Fryer remained on board the *I-165* for the remainder of its patrol before being taken to Penang and then on to Singapore, where he remained for the rest of the war. It is not quite clear as to why Fryer was spared whilst the other men were massacred. Out of a crew of sixty-two, only thirty-three survived. They were rescued on 22 March by the Royal Navy light cruiser HMS *Emerald* from four life rafts and were put ashore at Port Louis, Mauritius, on 26 March 1944.

When the war ended, the captain of submarine *I-165*, Lieutenant Shimizu, disappeared and was never brought to justice.

The MV *Behar*, a cargo ship of 8,000 tons captained by Maurice Symonds, left Melbourne, Australia on 19 February 1944, bound for the United Kingdom. It was due to call at Bombay and several other Indian ports before heading on to Southampton. The ship had a complement of 102, comprising 18 British officers, 67 Indian ratings, 15 Royal Artillery Maritime Regiment/DEMS gunners, and 2 Asdic operators. She also carried nine passengers.

The *Behar* was more heavily armed than most cargo ships in wartime, having one 4-inch and one 3-inch dual-purpose gun, a multiple rocket launcher, 20mm Oerlikons and a .5-inch Browning machine gun. In addition, and most unusual for a merchant ship, she was fitted with Asdic and carried depth charges.

On 9 March, some 340 miles north-west of the Cocos Islands in the Indian Ocean, the *Beha*r was spotted by the Japanese cruiser *Tone*, commanded by Captain Haruo Mayuzumi. The cruiser opened fire on the helpless ship, with shell after shell blasting great holes in her hull below the waterline. Such was the ferocity of the Japanese attack that the gunners on the *Behar* were unable to fire a single shot before the order was given to abandon ship. Two of the crew and a rating died in this attack. In all, 108 people managed to get away in four lifeboats – an amazing feat under such terrible bombardment.

The nearest land not occupied by the Japanese was Australia, 1,200 miles away. As they were debating what to do next, the *Tone* surfaced some 50 yards away and a message came across from a loudhailer in broken English ordering them to pull alongside. With Japanese sailors armed with guns on the decks, they had little choice but to obey. As the lifeboats pulled alongside, rope ladders were thrown over and the men ordered to climb aboard.

Once on the deck of the cruiser, they were bound tightly with ropes and an announcement in broken English came over the ship's tannoy system:

> You are now prisoners of Nippon. The Imperial Nipponese Forces are victorious in battle and will rid the Indian Ocean and Pacific of all Europeans. Because you have surrendered you are now number ten citizens. You will be treated well providing you obey the orders of your new masters. Water is being brought to you to cool you down.

Two Japanese sailors appeared carrying a 6-gallon container of water, and after placing it in front of the prisoners, they were given permission to shuffle forward to get some water. Awkwardly, because of the way they were bound, they moved forward, with an interpreter telling them: 'You will go down on your knees like animals do. No assistance will be given.'

Desperate to slake their thirsts, the first few knelt down before the water container and with lowered heads thrust forward, drank greedily. Screams filled the air when they discovered that the container was filled with seawater, to the amusement of the Japanese crew, who broke out into fits of laughter.

With their hands tied behind their backs and ropes around their necks, they were forced to sit on the deck in the baking hot sun for several hours before being herded down into a hold. When Petty Officer Phillips protested strongly and pointed out that this treatment was against the Geneva Convention, he was beaten with a baseball bat. The two women prisoners were released from their bonds and put in a separate room.

For six days they sat in the blisteringly hot hold with very little to eat or drink until the *Tone* arrived at the Javanese port of Tanjung Priok, where Captain Mayuzumi reported his success in sinking the *Behar* to Vice Admiral Sakonju, of the flagship *Aoba*. He was told by Sakonju that he was to keep thirty-five selected personnel and dispose of the rest by taking them back out to sea and executing them. Several European officers including Captain Symonds, twenty English-speaking seamen, along with seven passengers were picked out to remain at Tanjung Priok. The following evening, 18 March, the *Tone* put to sea, where the seventy-two remaining crewmembers, mainly lascars from Goa, were beheaded and their bodies dumped into the sea.

On 26 March 1944, the SS *Tjisalak*, a 5,787-ton Dutch freighter that was used to transport supplies between Australia and Ceylon, was sailing in the Indian Ocean bound for Colombo. It had a crew of eighty, comprising Dutch, Chinese and English merchant seamen, plus ten Royal Navy gunners manning the ship's 4-inch gun. Also on board were five passengers (including an American Red Cross nurse, Verna Gorden-Britten) and twenty-two lascar sailors.

At 0545 hrs the following morning, the *Tjisalak* was hit by a torpedo fired from the Japanese submarine *I-8*, commanded by Tatsunosuke Ariizumi. Captain Hen gave the order to abandon ship, but whilst most of the crew obeyed, taking to the life rafts, he himself, along with the British gunners, remained on board.

The 105 survivors were then taken aboard the submarine, where Captain Hen was taken into the conning tower to be interrogated. One of the Chinese sailors tried to escape by jumping into the sea, but as he tried to swim away, he was shot. The rest of the crew were tied in pairs on the deck of the submarine before being shot and pushed overboard.

Only five crewmembers survived the massacre: Chief Officer Frits de Jong, Second Officer Jan Dekker, Second Wireless Operator James Blears and Third Engineer Cees Spuybroek, and a lascar named Dhange.

These five men managed to swim back to where the *Tjisalak* had gone down, hoping to find an abandoned life raft. Their luck was in, as they found one in a reasonable state and after clambering on board, managed to drift for three days before being rescued by an American Liberty ship, the SS *James O. Wilder*. They were taken to Colombo, where they were able to tell the story of the sinking of the *Tjisalak* and the atrocities.

The commander of the submarine, Tatsunosuke Ariizumi, was classified as a war criminal, but he committed suicide in August 1945, avoiding the war crimes tribunals. This assertion has been disputed by historians who allege that he was put ashore in Tokyo Bay when the war ended, and simply vanished. Three members of his crew, however, were found guilty of war crimes, two serving prison terms whilst the third was granted immunity in exchange for testifying against his shipmates.

On 3 June 1944, a convoy of nineteen hell ships along with five escorts left Keppel Harbour, Singapore, bound for Japan. This convoy included the *Tamahoko Maru*, with 772 prisoners on board, most of whom had recently been transported to Singapore from Batavia. One of the men on board was an Irish Royal Air Force doctor called Aidan MacCarthy.

The convoy reached Manila in the Philippines without incident and headed on towards Japan across the East China Sea. As usual, conditions on board the *Tamahoko* were dreadful. Very little food and water was available, and the men were crammed into stifling holds. Doctor MacCarthy and his medical colleagues did their best to help many of the men who were in a very bad state.

Three weeks later, on the night of 24 June, as the convoy approached Japan, the US submarine *Tang* was lying in wait. Just before midnight, the *Tang* fired two torpedoes at the *Tamahoko*, one hitting just behind the bow and the second amidships. Water poured into the holds and within minutes, the ship went down. Doctor MacCarthy takes up the story in his book *A Doctor's War*:

> My first reaction was one of hopelessness as water was beginning to cascade into the hold, but thanks to my knowledge of the ship I knew where the hold inspection ladder was, so I made a desperate dash towards it. I jumped over the side and tried to put as much distance as possible between me and the rapidly sinking ship. From my vantage point on the surface of the water I saw the ship shudder and slide down into the sea. I took a deep breath as our ship plunged, expecting to be sucked down after it, but fortunately nothing happened, and I realised I was not going to die just yet. Cries and screams came from all around me. I could hear them even above the crackle of flames from a burning tanker. I clung to some floating wreckage in the heaving oily sea until dawn with a few of my colleagues.
>
> Around midday, after twelve hours in the sea, about twenty of us were picked up by a Japanese destroyer. We assumed that we would be treated well by the Japanese Navy, but they began to systematically beat us up and throw us overboard again. Helping each other in the sea those of us who had been lucky enough to survive swam back to the wreckage now some distance away. We decided to try and swim

to the Cheju Islands about eighteen miles away. A Japanese whaler picked us up and took us into Nagasaki harbour. There, the Japanese Army insisted that the captain of the whaler take us back out to sea and dump us overboard, but he refused. 560 out of the 772 prisoners who left Singapore perished.'

Another convoy of ships with almost 5,000 Allied prisoners on board left Singapore a few weeks later, on 4 July 1944. These ships were the *Asaka Maru*, the *Hakushika Maru*, the *Sekiho Maru*, the *Rashin Maru* and the *Hōfuku Maru*. John Wyatt of the East Surrey Regiment recalled the men being addressed by Lieutenant Colonel Nakamura in Singapore just before they boarded the ship:

> You are being transferred to the Holy Land of the Rising Sun, where scenery is simply superb. The land has four distinct seasons; Spring – with abundance of various blossoms, where birds chirp peaceful everywhere; evergreen Summer – with cool breezes easing the universe; transparent Autumn sky with clement moon; and with Winter, in which snow whitewashes the whole country, purifying the inhabitants. Therefore, I tell you, officers, and men, go to Japan with ease of mind and do your imposed duty to perfection. Then I verily tell you that our billion nationals will be welcoming you to share the imperial favour with you.
>
> On the other hand, should any one of you still retain conscience of any iniminal nationals, and project or proceed things up against to the interest of Japan, consequential results must be borne on his own shoulders, however regrettable to all concerned.
>
> In conclusion, I should like to call your attention to take good care of your health for the sudden change in climatical conditions and wish you the happy future.

'What a load rubbish,' John muttered to his mate Mick Shiels.

John also told me about his voyage on the *Asaka Maru* in an interview, later to be published in his book *No Mercy from the Japanese*:

> It was 4 July 1944 when this whole comical convoy of ten wrecks loaded with over 5,000 allied prisoners of war, set off for the land of the rising

sun. Conditions on board were by this time almost unbearable and every one of us was in a state of great physical and mental distress. The latrine was a large wooden box lashed to the side of the ship with an opening in the middle and a ledge on either side for your feet. With dysentery still rife there was always a constant queue to use this primitive contraption, with some men going up to fifteen times a day. Matters were made even worse as the inside of the box was slippery from the blood excreted by the dysentery sufferers. My bare feet would often slip as I squatted down, and I was terrified of being washed into the sea when a big wave broke, or the ship rolled. You had to hang on with all your strength. I saw one man tragically get washed away as he was so weak that he was unable to hang on. When we reported this to the Japanese guards, they just shrugged their shoulders and turned away, completely oblivious to our distress and suffering. We had no toilet paper and had to use what we could find or scrounge including pages from the few books left in our possession.

Malaria broke out again with a vengeance on board and as we had almost no quinine, we had to suffer the dreadful effects of this awful disease. Beri-beri was also on the increase. Many of my comrades were to die on this fateful voyage and we wrapped them in rice sacks and tipped them into the sea. Not even a prayer was said as they were consigned to a grave somewhere in the depths of the sea.

During the fifty-six days of that voyage at least twenty men died. Many more arrived in a perilous state, hanging onto their lives by a thread. I have no idea, some sixty-three years later, how my colleagues were affected by those two sea journeys to Japan, but I can tell you that even today when I close my eyes, I can still see that filthy, stinking hold, smell the stale odours of sick, shit, urine and death. I can still hear the cries for help from my fellow POWs.

Whilst Wyatt's journey on the *Asaka Maru* was dreadful, he was one of the lucky ones as around fifty prisoners died across all the ships in that convoy. Many more were to die on the ships that left for Japan over the following months.

On 2 July 1944, the American liberty ship *Jean Nicolet*, with 41 crew, 28 US Armed Guards and 31 passengers on board, was sunk by the Japanese submarine *I-8* while on her way from Freemantle, Australia, to Colombo in the Indian Ocean. The captain of the *I-8* was Commander Tatsunosuke Ariizumi, the same man who was in command when the *Tjisalak* was sunk, as outlined earlier in this chapter.

When the *Jean Nicolet* was hit by two torpedoes, the crew managed to launch their lifeboats just before it slipped under the waves. By now, the *I-8* had surfaced and Ariizumi ordered them by tannoy to swim to the submarine. Five men on one of the lifeboats slipped over the side into the water and managed to evade the clutches of the Japanese, but the other survivors were hauled on board the submarine, tied together and forced to sit on the deck. Then, one by one, they were led to the stern of the vessel between rows of Japanese sailors who beat them with iron bars and clubs before pushing them into the sea. The Japanese sailors then closed the hatches and when the submarine submerged, the thirty remaining survivors were simply washed overboard. A few managed to swim back to the burning hulk of the *Jean Nicolet* and launch a raft before the ship sank. Fortunately, twenty-three of them survived to be picked up by the Indian Navy trawler *Hoxa*. One of the men who survived, the ship's carpenter, recalled what had happened to one of them, an 18-year-old sailor called King. He said: 'I saw the Japanese bayoneting him in the stomach before throwing him over the side.' Another of the survivors, the first engineer, called Pyle, gave this account:

> Somewhere around midnight I was picked out and led aft, at which time I noticed that the deck guns were being secured and that thirty-five survivors of our vessel were still sitting on the submarine's deck. I then found out that the Japanese crew were employing a tactic somewhat like the old Indian practice of running the gauntlet and were forcing the survivors to pass between two lines of Japanese sailors, armed with clubs, iron bars and other blunt instruments, and when the victims reached the end, pushing or knocking them into the sea. Apparently, this process had been going on for some time before I was called out to take my turn, and I estimated that the gauntlet consisted of about thirteen to fourteen men. When I stopped for a second to take stock of the situation, I was struck a terrific blow at the base of my head which caused me to feel a sensation like a bouncing ball. From there on, I was pushed along through two lines of Japanese sailors who rained blows upon my head and body with various objects, which I was too stunned

> or dazed to identify, although I was later told by my doctor that I had been cut with a bayonet or sword in the process. When I reached the end of the gauntlet, I fell into what appeared to be a white foamy sea.

Able seaman McDougall, one of the survivors, also described what happened:

> When the submarine came alongside our raft, we slipped into the water on the far side and clung on. For a time, we could not see exactly what was happening, but we did see the submarine go astern and heard machine-gun fire ... later she came back in our direction and put a light on us. We then climbed back on to the raft and the submarine came alongside and threw a line to us. Hess was the first man on board, and I was the second. They would only let us come on board one at a time, amidships on the port side by the conning-tower. When I climbed on to the deck, I was told to remove my life jacket and to put up my hands. ... While my hands were raised one of the Japanese sailors spotted my watch. He pulled my hand down and took the watch off my wrist. Then he saw my ring and tried to get it off my finger, but it was too tight. He drew his knife and as he appeared to be about to cut my finger off, I managed to get the ring off and handed it to him. All but three of the survivors were taken on board the submarine.

Of the one hundred passengers and crew of the *Jean Nicolet*, only twenty-three survived to tell the story. The captain of submarine *I-8*, Tatsunosuke Ariizumi, was nicknamed 'The Butcher' by the British Royal Navy because of several other atrocities he had committed against Allied merchant crews, including the *Tjisalak*. Ariizumi committed suicide when Japan surrendered in August 1945, but three members of the *I-8*'s crew were found guilty of war crimes and prosecuted. Two were convicted and served prison terms, which were commuted by the Japanese government in 1955, whilst a third was granted immunity in exchange for testifying against his former shipmates.

On 6 September 1944, a convoy including the *Rakuyo Maru* left Singapore with 1,318 Allied prisoners on board bound for Japan. Six days into the voyage, at around 0500 hrs on 12 September, it was hit by torpedoes fired from the United States submarine *Sealion*. The first torpedo shattered the *Rakuyo*'s bow with the second one scoring a direct hit on the engine room.

Down in the dark and dismal holds, the prisoners, realising that the ship was doomed, clambered up the ladders and out onto the deck as quickly as possible. The sight that greeted them was of total chaos; the sea all around was on fire as an oil tanker travelling in the convoy had also been hit. With the Japanese crew having commandeered the lifeboats and kicking back any prisoner who tried to join them, they threw anything they could find that would float into the sea and then jumped in themselves.

Just before dusk, the Japanese frigates who had been accompanying the convoy sailed through the middle of the hundreds of survivors who were clinging to anything they could find, chopping them to pieces with their propellers.

As dawn broke the following morning, the prisoners who had survived the sinking and were clinging on to rafts and other bits of flotsam, tied them together, sharing out any food and water that was available. Sails were made from shirts, with bits of canvas stretched out to try to catch the rain. Some of the men even tried to catch fish by dangling their feet in the water as bait. Of course, eating any fish caught this way made them even thirstier, and with virtually no water available, some of them were so thirsty that they began to drink seawater, making them dangerously unstable and going crazy. Some even had to be killed by their mates to prevent them doing damage.

Some of the men drifting in the sea were picked up by Japanese escort vessels from the convoy. One ship took 157 men on board, but as they were hauled onto the deck, they were hit with rifle butts and batons before being allowed to sit near the bow. Despite this treatment, the Japanese crew fed them with biscuits and gave them water.

Others floating around on life rafts were not so lucky and after several days, many began to die of thirst and hunger. A few were so desperate for water that they resorted to urinating in each other's mouths, whist others tried to get blood from the men who had died by slitting their throats. Several tried to cut their own veins to get blood to drink.

The *Kachidoki Maru*, with 900 British prisoners of war on board, which had left Singapore on 6 September in the same convoy as the *Rakuyo Maru*, managed to survive for another eighteen hours by zigzagging. Its luck was not to last, however, as just before midnight it too was hit by torpedoes from the *Growler* and *Sealion*. Within half an hour it had slipped below the waves, 476 prisoners losing their lives, all drowned in the holds. Those who survived and managed to get into the sea were left clinging on to lifeboats crammed with desperate men and lying dangerously low in the water. One lifeboat had sixty people on it with around seventy-five more hanging on to the sides. Any other men who swam up to it and tried to get on board were punched and kicked away.

The survivors of the *Kachidoki Maru* were the first to be rescued by the ships in the convoy that had not been sunk by the US submarines, and on the morning of the 13th, they were taken on board Japanese frigates that had arrived in the area from Hainan.

On the afternoon of the 15th, when the US submarine *Pampanito* discovered wreckage, the captain, Commander Paul Summers, was astonished to find life rafts with men still on them. Thinking that they were Japanese, he ordered his men to stand by with guns at the ready, but as the submarine got nearer to one of the life rafts, the crew heard a shout from one of them and closed in on it with their guns primed. They were still convinced the men were Japanese, and when the commander shouted out 'Do any of you speak English?', one of the men shouted back: 'You dumb bastards, we all speak English.' Still not convinced, he ordered only one man to come aboard. This man was called Frank Farmer, and he said: 'I was hauled across the intervening water to the sub's side, up which I was assisted by two crewmen. When I thanked them in English, they were incredulous.'

The crew of the *Pampanito* were astonished at the condition of the men, many so weak that they couldn't climb aboard. Most of them were covered in oil from the sunken tanker and it was difficult for the American crew to pull them on board. One crewmember said, 'It was like trying to capture a greased pig.'

As the men were hauled aboard, one shouted out: 'I'm a British prisoner of his Imperial Majesty the Emperor of Japan.' The crewmember said, 'No you're not, you're now a free man on a United States submarine.' A broad grin spread across the man's face.

By now, the *Sealion* had also joined in the search for survivors, picking up several more from life rafts before dusk fell. The *Pampanito* eventually rescued seventy-three men and the *Sealion* another fifty-four. Unfortunately, many other life rafts simply drifted away into the darkness, never to be seen again.

At around the same time, the *Shin'yō Maru*, with 750 prisoners on board, left Davao City in the Philippines in convoy C-076. There were 9 vessels in the convey, including 2 torpedo boats, 2 tankers, and 4 other medium and small cargo ships, bound for Manila.

About 2 or 3 miles off the Zamboanga Peninsula on the Philippine island of Mindanao, the convoy was attacked by the US submarine *Paddle*, under the command of Captain Byron Nowell. The *Paddle* fired two torpedoes, both striking the *Shin'yō*. It did not sink immediately, but the Japanese crew were so incensed that they opened the hatches and tossed grenades down into the holds packed with prisoners. Some of the prisoners who managed to escape this carnage flung themselves into the sea, whilst others were mowed down on the decks as they tried to escape. The Japanese then turned their guns onto the men struggling in the sea. One of the survivors of the massacre, US Marine Corps Sergeant Clem, later reported:

> Up on the bridge there was a machine gun spraying the hatch. A burst of machine-gun fire caught all three of us and knocked us back down in the hold. We'd all been hit. I got plowed in the skull. Another bullet chipped out my chin. Nevertheless, I was able to work myself back up on deck, and I was eyeing that bridge when I came out that time. The gun was still there, but the gunner was laying out on deck. Somebody had apparently got up there and killed him. At this time, I found out that we were out in the ocean about two or three miles from shore. All I had was a loincloth.

Out of the 750 Allied prisoners of war on board the *Shin'yō*, 668 were killed and only 82 managed to escape, reaching the shores of Sindangan Bay, where they received aid from friendly Filipino guerrillas.

On 15 September 1944, the *Jun'yō Maru*, with 6,520 prisoners on board, mostly from the 10th Battalion of Infantry in Batavia, along with civilians and personnel from the Merchant Navy, Ambonese and Manadonese soldiers from the Royal Dutch Indies Army, was moored up just outside the harbour of Tanjung Priok, a district of North Jakarta, Indonesia. The *Jun'yō* was bound for Padang, some 900 miles up the west coast of Sumatra.

As the ship sat just outside the harbour for twenty-four hours, the men sitting on the decks were subjected to blazing heat from the sun, whilst those in the holds were almost suffocating. One prisoner, who could take it no more, jumped overboard and made for the shore. His escape attempt was not to last long as he was quickly picked up by a Japanese lifeboat and heavily beaten. This was a warning to the rest of the prisoners as to what might happen if they attempted to escape.

A rust bucket of a ship, with only two small lifeboats along with several life rafts, the *Jun'yō* had almost no sanitary facilities, the men having to defecate and urinate on the deck or over the side. Because of overcrowding, it sometimes took an hour for them to reach the deck to relieve themselves.

The following day, 16 September at 1500 hrs, the *Jun'yō* eventually left Tanjung Priok escorted by two small gunboats and headed out into the Sunda Strait.

Two days into the journey, on 18 September, it was spotted by the British submarine HMS *Tradewind*, commanded by Lieutenant Commander S.L.C. Maydon. Maydon ordered four torpedoes to be launched at the *Jun'yō,* two of them hitting their target. The ship didn't sink immediately, but realising that it was going down, many of the prisoners who were on the decks jumped into the sea. Those still down in the holds were trapped.

Twenty minutes later, the *Jun'yō*'s stern went under, the bow rose into the air, and it sunk, taking the prisoners still trapped in the holds with it. The men who managed to survive clung on to lifeboats and any loose flotsam and jetsam, to avoid being sucked down with the ship.

The two gunboats in the convoy picked up the Japanese survivors first, before rescuing some of the prisoners, but any who were in a bad state or injured were simply left to drown. Those who survived were forced to sit on the decks of the gunships without food or anything to drink until they reached the coast, where they were forced to jump into the sea around a quarter of a mile from the beach and swim ashore. Of the 6,520 prisoners who boarded the *Jun'yō,* 5,640 died – by far the greatest number of any single ship sinking during the Second World War.

On 22 November 1944, the British submarine HMS *Stratagem*, commanded by Lieutenant Clifford Raymond Pelly, DSC, RN was patrolling off south-west Malaya. At around noon, the submarine was hit by depth charges dropped from a Japanese submarine chaser, *CH-35*.

The first depth charge caused Stratagem's bow to hit the sea bottom and caused flooding. The forward watertight bulkhead could not be closed, and she was forced to surface. Only ten of the crew of fifty-six managed to escape.

One of the crewmembers, Sidney Gibbs, recalled the attack:

> Almost immediately a depth-charge exploded somewhere extremely close under us, lifting the stern, and causing us to hit bottom hard. This charge extinguished the greater part of the lighting although one or two of the emergency lights held. About five seconds later a second charge exploded, as far as I could calculate, right amidships, extinguishing the remaining lights. By this time, I had a torch in operation and could see water flooding through the door at the after end of the torpedo stowage compartment. Immediately I gave the order 'Shut water-tight doors' and turned to make sure that the three ratings in the tube space were brought out of that compartment before the door was shut. By the time this door was shut, the water was flooding very much faster and had risen above the deck boards in the torpedo stowage compartment. It was now above our knees. It was flooding through the after door so fast that the ratings were unable to shut this door. The position of the stop (retaining door in 'open' position) on this water-tight door was such that to remove it one had to stand in the doorway as the port side of the door was blocked by stores. Hence, due to the furious rate of flooding, this stop could not be removed.

The Japanese destroyer then launched a cutter to pick up the ten survivors, most of whom were suffering from 'the bends', the decompression illness after a quick ascend.

Gibbs also recalled their treatment by the Japanese on board the destroyer:

> On being hauled on board we were bound, blindfolded, and beaten. We were not given food at any time whilst on board the destroyer and spent the night on the top of the hatch, which was about three feet square, all bound together. We were not clothed, and the night was extremely cold. The pain from the 'bends' was now at its worst and every time someone spoke, the guards would come and hit us over the head with their clubs.

Only Gibbs and two others out of the ten survivors managed to survive captivity.

On 14 December 1944, the *Ōryoku Maru* left Manila in the Philippines bound for Japan. On board were 1,600 American and British prisoners, along with 1,500 Japanese troops, 547 Japanese civilians, and 1,127 crewmen and passengers from other shipwrecked Japanese vessels.

The prisoners were divided into three groups and forced down into holds, which had no light or ventilation, making it difficult for them to breathe. Initially, the hatches were left open to provide some light and air, but when the men began screaming for food and water, the Japanese guards ignored their requests and slammed the hatches shut.

The ship eventually got underway at about 0300 hrs, after the men had been cooped up in the holds without food or water for more than twenty-four hours. One of the prisoners, Commander Frank Bridget, a US Navy pilot, managed to persuade the Japanese to open the hatches again and allow small groups of men up on the deck for some fresh air. Eventually, food was provided, the Japanese crew lowering buckets into the holds containing a seaweed-rice mixture, but as it was pitch black, the men had no idea of what they were about to eat. The buckets were also to be used as toilets.

During the second night at sea, around fifty men died. Desperate for water, some of them even drank the blood of those who had died, whilst others drank their own urine to try to alleviate their thirst. Some licked condensation off the sides of the ship, whilst others drank the sewage that sloshed in the bottom of the holds.

The following morning, the bodies of the fifty men who had died during the night were removed from the holds and simply flung over the side. More buckets of fish and steamed rice were lowered down into the holds, but still no water was provided. Later that day, aircraft from Task Force 38's *Hornet* and *Hancock* found the *Ōryoku* heading north, just to the west of the Bataan Peninsula and attacked it. Several of the Japanese crew were injured and two American doctors were summoned from the holds to treat them. Despite providing help, the doctors were later beaten with gun butts and bamboo sticks.

Although badly damaged, the *Ōryoku* managed to limp along slowly and head for the shelter of Subic Bay, on the west side of Luzon, where the Japanese soldiers and civilians disembarked. The prisoners were left locked in the holds without food or water for another night. Some of them were so desperate that they broke into stores looking for food. A Japanese lieutenant who found them shot one of them and herded the others back into the holds.

One of the American prisoners who survived, Loren E. Stamp, recalled the horrors of that night they were left locked in the holds at Subic Bay:

'More men were killed to keep them from killing others in their frenzy. Still more tried to kill themselves.'

Even in the shelter of Subic Bay, the Japanese were fully aware that the ship was still in grave danger and could be bombed again at any time. The officer in charge of the prisoners considered leaving them locked in the holds to die from the bombs of their fellow countrymen, but fortunately, he relented and allowed them up on deck. They were told by the officer that they would have to swim ashore, about 300 yards away:

> No shoes only shirts and pants to wear. Must leave packs but can take food kit and canteen. Japanese soldiers very good with guns. Will kill any man who tries to escape. All men be very careful. You go twenty-five at one time. Must swim to land.

At around 0830 hrs, as they prepared to make their way up onto the decks to swim ashore, a wave of American bombers swept in dropping their bombs on the ship. One landed near the aft hold, where around 300 men were killed. About ten minutes later, as it all went quiet up on the decks, some of the prisoners cautiously raised the hatches to discover that the crew had abandoned ship and there was no sign of life. It was now a mad stampede up the ladders onto the decks, where they discovered the bodies of Japanese soldiers and civilians, including children, lying everywhere.

As the ship was on fire, with ammunition exploding, they wasted no time in diving overboard and swimming towards the nearby shore. When the first group reached land, they realised that there was no beach to crawl up, just a 4-foot seawall, and sitting on the wall were Japanese soldiers with machine guns. Many of the first group of men were mowed down as they tried to climb up outside the designated area that had been set up. Of course, the men had no idea about the area to where they were supposed to swim.

Lieutenant Colonel Montgomery, one of the survivors, gave the following account of the sinking and subsequent acts of violence:

> In the hold, we were informed that we would have to swim for shore. We were ordered not to take our shoes and to strip down as much as possible. On ascending the ladders, some of the men were permitted to go to one of the lower levels and jump overboard. Others were forced to jump from right where they were, a drop of eighteen feet. The Japanese

guards on board were trigger-happy, and several people were shot while on board. Machine guns were lined up on the shore, which opened up on men on improvised rafts.

Those who survived and managed to make it ashore were forced onto a concrete square that had once been used as a tennis court. By now, there were only 1,333 prisoners left alive out of the original 1,600, and more were dying each day. It was blisteringly hot during the day and freezing cold at night, as they had no shelter.

Five days later, the Japanese loaded the men into trucks and took them to San Fernando, Pampanga, where they were put in a gaol that was a converted cinema. Some of them jokingly asked 'When does the film start?'

Fifteen of the sickest men were taken away on the pretext that they were being taken to hospital in Manila, but they were simply taken to a cemetery, where they were bayoneted and decapitated.

At the Yokohama War Crimes Trials in 1945, Junsaburo Toshino, Guard Commandant aboard the *Ōryoku*, was found guilty of murdering at least sixteen men, and sentenced to death as a Class B war criminal. The captain of the ship, Shin Kajiyama, was acquitted, 'as he had no chance to prevent any atrocities'.

In early July 1945, with the war nearing its end, ninety civilian prisoners including women and children were marched on board a Japanese submarine in the port of Cheribon (now Cirebon) in northern Java. The submarine set sail, travelling on the surface with the prisoners sitting on the deck. The women and children were frightened as they clung to each other as the vessel moved through the gently rolling sea. After sailing for about an hour, the submarine suddenly dived without warning, sweeping the terrified prisoners into the sea. Schools of sharks attacked the screaming mass of humanity as the men, women and children were torn to pieces in a feeding frenzy. Only one person, minus an arm and right foot, survived to be rescued by a Javanese fisherman. He was able to tell his story to the crew of the fishing boat before he died a short time later. His body was committed to the sea, as the three fishermen were fully aware of their fate should they return to port with the body of a European on board.

After the war, this atrocity was reported to the authorities but as all naval files and records of ship movements had been destroyed by the Japanese, the identity of the submarine and its crew was never established.

When the war ended, many of the captains and crew of the hell ships were charged with war crimes for their mistreatment of Allied prisoners of war, but many simply vanished.

Captain Odake Bunji, in charge of the *Asaka Maru*, and Lieutenant Ino Takeo were charged with the ill-treatment of prisoners due to gross overcrowding, improper sanitation, and lack of food, drinking water and medical supplies on board. They were also charged with a lack of safety precautions for attacks, given that there was no indication that the ship was carrying prisoners of war. Both defendants were found guilty and sentenced to terms of imprisonment.

Chapter 11
Murder of Aircrews
April 1942–July 1945

On 18 April 1942, at around midday, sixteen US Army bombers, led by Lieutenant Colonel Jimmy Doolittle, took off from the aircraft carrier *Hornet* in the Pacific. Their targets were Tokyo and other towns on Honshu, the largest and most populous island of Japan, in retaliation for the Japanese attack on Pearl Harbor four months earlier. It was the first American air operation of the war to strike the Japanese archipelago.

After they had carried out their attacks and dropped their bombs, the planes flew on to China, where, after running out of fuel, the crews bailed out or crashed along the coastline. Most of the aircrews were rescued and hidden by local Chinese people, including guerrillas and missionaries, many of whom were to pay the price for hiding them as a considerable number of men, women and children were slaughtered in retaliation.

The Japanese were so incensed by the Doolittle raids that, on 13 August, they passed the 'Enemy Airmen's Act', which stated: 'Allied pilots who bomb non-military targets in the Pacific Theatre and are captured on land or at sea by Japanese forces will be subject to trial and punishment.' It decreed that any American airman who bombed Japan would be subject to be sentenced to death for the following offences: 1. on ordinary people; 2. on private property of a non-military nature; 3. against other than military objectives; 4. violations of wartime international law.

Once captured, the airmen's status as prisoners often remained rather ambiguous. They could be detained as criminals, spies, saboteurs, or terrorists depending on what their targets were deemed to be, or until their Japanese captors determined what treatment they (often subjectively) deemed appropriate. This Enemy Airmen's Act was to contribute to the deaths of hundreds of Allied airmen throughout the Pacific War. It has been estimated that 132 Allied airmen who were shot down during the bombing campaign against the Japanese islands in 1944–45 were summarily executed after short kangaroo trials.

During the Battle of Midway in June 1942, three American airmen who had been shot down were taken on board a Japanese warship. After being interrogated they were executed, their bodies tied to 5-gallon kerosene cans filled with water and dumped overboard from the ship.

In early July 1942, two sets of aircrews who made forced landings in China at around the same time were captured by the Japanese. One crew was taken to Shanghai and the other to Nanking, where they were interrogated and tortured. A week later, despite being in a bad state, they were taken to Tokyo, where they were imprisoned in the Kempeitai headquarters, where they were forced to sign written statements in Japanese, which of course they could not understand, before being taken back to Shanghai. At the end of July, eight of them were put on trial, where none of the accusations directed at them were in English and they had no defence. Three were sentenced to death whilst the other five were given life imprisonment.

Details of these early massacres of American aircrews did not become public in the United States until April 1943, when President Roosevelt issued the following statement to the American people:

> It is with a feeling of deepest horror, which I know will be shared by all civilized peoples, that I must announce the barbarous execution by the Japanese government of some of the members of this country's armed forces who fell into Japanese hands as an incident of warfare. The press has just carried the details of the American bombing of Japan a year ago. The crews of two of the American bombers were captured by the Japanese. On 19 October 1942, this Government learned from Japanese radio broadcasts of the capture, trial, and severe punishment of those Americans. Continued endeavour was made to obtain confirmation of those reports from Tokyo. It was not until 12 March 1943 that the American government received the communication given by the Japanese government stating that these Americans had in fact been tried and that the death penalty had been pronounced against them. It was further stated that the death penalty was commuted for some but that the sentence of death had been applied to others.
>
> This Government has vigorously condemned this act of barbarity in a formal communication sent to the Japanese government. In that communication this Government has informed the Japanese government

> that the American government will hold personally and officially responsible for these diabolical crimes all of those officers of the Japanese government who have participated therein and will in due course bring those officers to justice.
>
> This recourse by our enemies to frightfulness is barbarous. The effort of the Japanese warlords thus to intimidate us will utterly fail. It will make the American people more determined than ever to blot out the shameless militarism of Japan.
>
> I have instructed the Department of State to make public the text of our communication to the Japanese.

This proclamation to the American people strengthened their resolve to defeat the Japanese using any means possible.

In March 1944, sixty-two American airmen who were shot down during bombing raids on Rabaul, Papua New Guinea, were taken prisoner by the Japanese forces there. They were locked up in a former tailor's shop by the 6th Field Kempeitai, before being taken the following day to a beach, where they were crammed into a small cave with hardly any room to move. For two days, they were not given any food, just a couple of buckets of water to drink, water that the Japanese guards had washed their dishes in. They were then told that they were to be transferred to a camp on Watom Island, 6 miles offshore, where they were massacred by the Japanese guards. According to Japanese reports at the end of the war, they were all killed by friendly fire during a bombing raid and their bodies cremated on a huge funeral pyre on the beach. At the war crimes trials, this was disproven and it was revealed that they had been deliberately massacred by their Japanese guards.

On 2 September 1944, an American aircraft with nine airmen on board was shot down near the Bonin Islands, also known as the Ogasawara Islands, an archipelago some 650 miles directly south of Tokyo and 1,000 miles north-west of Guam. The crew of eight were captured by the Japanese, with only one man escaping, that man being no other than former American President George H.W. Bush. Floating in the water for four hours, Bush was eventually rescued by the submarine USS *Finback*. The other unlucky crewmembers who had been captured were tortured, stabbed and beheaded before being cannibalised. Admiral Mori Kunizo, who oversaw the Chichi-Jima base at the time, confirmed this by testifying at the end of the war: 'A chef had [the liver] pierced with bamboo sticks and cooked with soy sauce and vegetables, we believed it to be good for the stomach.'

It wasn't until 2003 that George Bush found out that he too could have been served on the same plate as his unfortunate comrades.

Kunizo was found guilty of war crimes and sentenced to life imprisonment for the cannibalism of American airmen on Chichi-Jima, the largest and most populous island in the Bonin Islands. He was later hanged by the Dutch for atrocities he also committed in the Netherlands East Indies earlier in the war.

Another Japanese senior officer found guilty of the cannibalism of US airmen was Lieutenant General Yoshio Tachibana. After a trial in August 1946, he was sentenced to death and hanged.

From October 1944 until May 1945, fourteen US airmen, aged between 19 and 24, were shot down during raids over Taiwan. The airmen were held in Taihoku (Taipei) Prison, where they were tortured and beaten. On 29 May, they were tried under the Enemy Airman's Act, found guilty and sentenced to death.

Three weeks later, on 19 June, they were executed by firing squad in the courtyard of the prison. Their bodies were cremated, with their ashes kept in a local Japanese temple until the end of the war, when they were handed over to the American War Graves recovery team.

When the war ended, a former commander of the Taiwan army and Governor General called Rikichi Andō, along with his aide Major Shozo Matsuo and eight others, was arrested and charged with war crimes in China and Taiwan. After their arrest, they were sent to Ward Road Gaol in Shanghai for trial by the war crimes tribunal. Four days later, Andō committed suicide by taking a potassium cyanide capsule that he had hidden in a tube of toothpaste. Major Matsuo also committed suicide by hanging himself in his cell.

The other eight were all found guilty, two being sentenced to death and six sentenced to terms of imprisonment.

In early February 1945, an RAF Liberator crashed in Burma. The crew of six were captured by the Japanese and imprisoned at Myanaung on the Irrawaddy River, where they were interrogated by the Kempeitai. Refusing to give any information to their captors, they were marched to some open ground, where a group of Japanese guards was waiting for them. All six airmen were led to the side of a newly dug trench, blindfolded, bound and forced to sit on the edge before being beheaded by a Japanese officer. The guards then carried out bayonet practice on the headless bodies.

In late March 1945, two American airmen were taken prisoner after they had been shot down over Cebu in the Philippines. Without any form of trial, they were taken to a piece of wasteland near a school, where they were decapitated, and their bodies kicked into trenches. Wood was piled on top of the bodies, and they were incinerated.

With the war now going against them and air attacks becoming more frequent, the Japanese became even more violent towards captured airmen. On 15 April 1945, an American B-29 bomber was shot down with only three crewmembers surviving after parachuting to the ground. After being taken prisoner, the three airmen were grilled by Japanese officers, before two were beheaded and one killed with a bayonet. Their bodies were cremated, with their ashes dumped into the sea.

During May 1945, as the war entered its final phase, the Allies launched bombing attacks on Tokyo. During the attacks, several aircraft were shot down, with sixty-two Allied airmen taken prisoner and incarcerated along with 464 Japanese soldiers who were under sentence. A few days later, the prison buildings, made primarily of wood, were hit by incendiary bombs and completely destroyed. At the Tokyo War Crimes Tribunals, it was discovered that all of the 464 Japanese soldiers in the prison had survived, and the airmen had been executed in revenge for the attacks. It seemed too much of a coincidence for them to be unlucky, as they had been housed in the same building as the Japanese prisoners.

An American airman who was shot down near Saigon in May 1945 was taken prisoner and locked up in the Kempeitai gaol. He had been badly burned but received no medical treatment for three days, during which time he was interrogated despite being in severe pain. Eventually, he was taken to a military hospital where, despite being on his way to recovery, a fatal dose of novocaine was injected into his jugular vein: he died in less than two minutes. The three doctors concerned, along with a Kempeitai captain, were tried by a British Military Court after the war and all four were sentenced to death by hanging.

Also in May 1945, during a bombing attack on Kyushu, another B-29 was shot down, with eleven crewmembers bailing out and landing close to the town of Fukuoka. The airmen were captured and taken to Kyushu University, where they were told they were going to receive treatment for their injuries.

This was not to be, as the Japanese medics decided to use them as guinea pigs for experiments. One crewmember was shot in the stomach so that medical students could practise removing bullets from a person still alive. Another crewmember was injected with seawater to find out if it could be a substitute for saline solution. Another had a part of his brain removed in a test for epilepsy. These experiments were carried out under the command of Professor Ishiyama Fukujiro, director of external medicine. In one experiment he cut out an airman's lungs, and after making a cut into the lung artery, blood flowed into his thorax, killing him instantly. Others had their livers removed to see how long a person could live without one. Ishiyama also removed a prisoner's stomach before blocking an artery near the heart to see how long he could survive. The pilot of the B-29, Captain Marvin Watkins, had been transferred to Tokyo for interrogation and managed to survive the gruesome experiments.

A Japanese doctor called Toshio Tono, a first-year student at the Kyushu University who was present during the experiments outlined above, has dedicated himself to ensuring that the experiments on the eight airmen should never be forgotten. After the war, Tono was so appalled about what happened that he could not bear to be in the company of other doctors. He then committed himself to bringing this atrocity into the public eye as one of the darkest periods of Japan's modern history. Tono recalls:

> One day two blindfolded airmen were brought to the school in a truck and taken to the pathology lab. Two soldiers stood guard outside the room. I did wonder if something unpleasant was going to happen to them, but I had no idea it was going to be that awful.

As a trainee medical student, one of Tono's jobs was to wash the blood from the floor and to prepare saline drips. He asserts:

> The experiments had no medical merit, they were being used to inflict as cruel a death as possible on the prisoners. I was in a state of panic, but I couldn't say anything to the other doctors. We kept being reminded of the misery US bombing raids had caused in Japan. But looking back it was a terrible thing to have happened. The way Japan was during the war, it was impossible to refuse orders from the military. Dr Ishiyama and the other doctors committed crimes, but in a way they were also

> victims of the war. But I hated doctors for a while. I couldn't get to sleep without pills.

Many of the bodies were preserved in formaldehyde to be used later by students, but when the war ended, the bodies were cremated to hide any evidence of the atrocities.

Tono also recalls removing eyeballs from the bodies to keep for future experiments and research. After the war, he spent years examining documents and revisiting relevant locations in an attempt to establish what had happened. Ignoring pleas from his former superiors not to disclose the truth about the atrocities, he went ahead with his memoirs.

Kyushu University doctors and military staff stood trial after the war on 11 March 1948. Thirty people, including several doctors and one female nurse, were convicted of vivisection, the removal of body parts and cannibalism. The charges of cannibalism were dropped, but twenty-three were found guilty of vivisection or wrongful removal of body parts. Five were sentenced to death and another four to life imprisonment, and the rest to shorter terms. One of the most senior doctors, Fukujiro Ishiyama, killed himself after the war. When the Korean War started in June 1950, General Douglas MacArthur reduced most of the sentences. The death sentences were never carried out. All were released by 1958.

The Japanese often ordered the cremation of captured aircrews' remains after their execution, many of which were then dispersed at sea in an attempt to conceal the crimes.

Towards the end of the war, when aircrews were shot down over the Japanese home islands, they were often captured by local people. There are numerous personal accounts of downed airmen who survived, reporting that they experienced mistreatment at the hands of angry civilians once they parachuted to the ground. An American airman, 2nd Lieutenant Fiske Hanley, who was shot down during a raid near the Shimonoseki Straits on 27 March 1945, stated in his memoirs:

> I descended near the small village of Ueki, where a large crowd of forty to fifty angry and armed farmers immediately surrounded me after I landed in a rice paddy. One of the Japanese men, holding a bamboo spear, charged at me from my right front. His spear was levelled at my head.

> At his signal, the others joined in his charge. I reached out and deflected his spear over my head. He lunged passed me! Then the excited horde was upon me. They were like a pack of crazed and starved animals after raw meat. They were so close that they couldn't use their larger weapons. They became a mass of jammed humanity as they milled around me. I was hit with fists and clubs. They hit me from every direction. Their main target seemed to be my head, and they didn't miss. My flak suit and survival gear gave me some protection and probably saved my vitals from severe wounds. Lack of a helmet made my head fair game. I tried to parry the vicious jabs at my eyes. Fortunately, no one had a knife. The women were especially vicious. There was no reprieve from the attack. I was being clubbed and beaten to death. These savages had no thought of allowing me to surrender. Capture was not in their minds. They were out to kill me! The mob was in a frenzy and out of control. No one seemed to be in charge. Their shouting increased in tempo as they – men, women, and children – fought to get in lethal blows. I used my bloody hands and arms to protect my head, which was already burned from my bailout from the flaming airplane. I was bleeding profusely, my shirt soaked with blood. My instinct to live was foremost in my mind, but I was losing that battle. A figure several rows back in the mob managed to severely poke my face on the right cheekbone with an implement shaft of some kind. An inch above and it would have put out an eye. I was knocked down countless times and each time struggled to my feet. I never lost consciousness during the beating. This was a horrible way to die! By now, I was believing I had made the wrong decision. I should have shot myself. I kept yelling 'I surrender!' and prayed. Fortunately, a local police officer intervened, and my life was saved.

Concerned now about such treatment by the public, the Japanese government generally tried to keep strict control over civilians. One such incident that highlights this occurred on 8 August 1945 – two days after the atomic bomb was dropped on Hiroshima – and involved the last B-29 shot down during the Second World War. Its crew crash-landed near Tachikawa, 25 miles west of Tokyo, following a bombing mission against the Nakajima aircraft factory. Two crewmen, Lester C. Morris and Serafino Morone, managed to bail out of the plummeting aircraft and parachute safely to the ground, where they were captured and taken to the Tachikawa Kempeitai headquarters. Upon their arrival, they were confronted by a large mob of Japanese civilians who shouted and spat at them, but they were not mistreated, although later, they were to be tortured by the Kempeitai. Morris was to survive to tell his story after the war ended, but Morone was not so lucky. This is Morris's account of what happened to them:

> Despite the fact that I was already in bad shape when captured, they beat me during questioning so much that I lost consciousness three times. Each time they brought me back to consciousness with buckets of cold water and continued the treatment. I believe they must have done worse to Morone because of the secret radio codes he may have possessed.

An account of what happened to Morone was outlined in the Review by the Staff Judge Advocate, on 8 October 1948, in the United States:

> The following day, Major Shichisaburo Yajima (Kempeitai) decided it would be best to put the airman (Morone) on display since a large number of people wanted to see a captured airman as it would be a way to bolster the spirit among the populace to continue the war. Kempeitai officials arranged to use the grounds of a nearby school, as it provided more room to accommodate the large crowd. Fully aware that this incident would result in his death, officials then sought and received permission from the city council to dispose of his remains in the public burial grounds. At around 1300 hrs, three guards escorted him to the schoolyard, followed by a large crowd that had been notified in advance of the opportunity for revenge. Morone was reportedly only wearing pants, which were torn below the knees, and was blindfolded with his hands tied together. Once at the schoolyard, guards tied him to a post with his back toward the crowd. The guards displayed a sign that read: 'This flyer was one of the persons who bombed Tokyo, and because of the bombings, we have lost our loved ones, brothers, and sisters, and you will wreak your revenge upon this person.' A guard, W/O Noboru Seki, then addressed the crowd, stating 'Ladies and gentlemen, you will now be permitted to beat this B-29 flyer. However, each one will only strike the prisoner one time.' Although several members of the crowd came prepared with large clubs, guards insisted they use a split

> bamboo stick, to prolong the torture and prevent immediate death. As the beating began, the crowd had allegedly grown to well over 1,000 people, several hundred of whom (including women) lined up to beat the unfortunate airman. The public display lasted nearly two hours and was only stopped due to an air raid alarm at around 1,600 hrs. Clearly suffering in pain throughout the ordeal, witnesses reported that Morone was delirious and that guards gave him water now and then to revive him, only to continue the beating. As the crowd eventually dispersed, guards placed him on a stretcher, as he was far too weak to walk, and carried him to the cemetery, where his grave had already been dug. They placed him next to the grave and an officer approached, drew his sword, and decapitated him. Morone's body fell into the grave, which was quickly filled in.

Afterwards, Kempeitai officials requested that a doctor, called Nakayama, fill out a death certificate for Morone in which it stated that he had died from injuries sustained in the crash of his B-29 and was completely burned.

During the war crimes tribunals held after the war, around 394 Japanese military were charged with unlawful torture, execution, and mutilation of the bodies of airmen. The victims included over 400 American airmen, nearly all of whom were killed.

Chapter 12

The Sandakan Death Marches

March 1945

The island of Borneo was a key strategic target for the Japanese after Pearl Harbor and the invasion of Malaya. On 18 December 1941, using small fishing boats, they landed forces at Sandakan on Sabah's north-east coast, the seat of government in British North Borneo.

By the end of the month, the entire island had fallen into Japanese hands, with little opposition from either the British or the Dutch colonial governments.

Six months later, on 7 July, 1,500 prisoners of war, mostly Australians taken at the fall of Singapore under the command of Lieutenant Colonel A.W. Walsh, were transported to Sandakan to build an airfield. They were loaded onto a decrepit tramp steamer, the *Yubi Maru* (sometimes known as the *Ume Maru*). Conditions on the ship were dreadful, and as it had originally transported coal, everything was covered in a black dust that seeped into the pores of the men.

When the *Yubi Maru* docked at Sandakan on 18 July, some of the prisoners spent the night sleeping in a church, whilst others slept on a padang or on the ship. The following morning, they were counted, given a meagre breakfast and marched 10 miles to Number 1 Prisoner of War Camp, a facility that had previously been used as a Royal Air Force base. The Japanese officer in charge of the camp, Lieutenant Hoshijima Susumi, addressed the prisoners shortly after they arrived:

> You have been brought here to Sandakan to have the honour to build for the Imperial Japanese forces an aerodrome. For this you will be paid ten cents a day. You will work. You will build this aerodrome if it takes three years. I tell you I have the power of life and death over you. You will build this aerodrome if you stay here until your bones rot under the Borneo sun.

For the first few months, as security in the camp was lax, several prisoners managed to escape into the jungle. The Japanese then clamped down, the prisoners having their already inadequate food supplies drastically reduced for a week as a deterrent. They were threatened with death should anyone else try to escape.

Work on the airfield progressed slowly for the next nine months until, in April 1943, more prisoners of war, mainly British, arrived to bolster a workforce that now amounted to around 2,750 men. To help speed up progress, the Japanese brought in a group of experienced army guards. These men were nicknamed the 'bashers', and they took great pleasure in beating the prisoners with wooden pick handles or bamboo canes to make them work harder. One of the Australian prisoners working on the airstrip, Jim Milner, was punished by the guards on many occasions. He recalls: 'We had to bow to all the Japanese officers, which was very degrading. And any Japanese, no matter what his rank, could bash you if he felt like it, and they used to take great delight in it.'

Things were to get worse in the camp when two of the prisoners, Captain Lionel Matthews and Lieutenant Rod Wells, managed to build a small radio. When it was discovered, they were arrested and tortured for several days. As Matthews was classed as the instigator, he was shot. Wells, who was reprieved and survived, recalled the torture in an interview he gave after the war:

> The interviewer produced a small piece of wood like a meat skewer, pushed that into my left ear, and tapped it in with a small hammer. I think I fainted sometime after it went through the drum. I remember the last excruciating sort of pain, and I must have gone out for some time because I was revived with a bucket of water. Eventually it healed but of course I couldn't hear with it. I have never been able to hear since.

Life was now very difficult for the remaining 2,434 prisoners in Sandakan; even very sick men were forced at bayonet point to work on the airstrip to get it completed to the time schedule set. The eighteen months that followed was to be hell on earth for them, but worse was to come.

By January 1945, around 534 men had died, with only 1,900 left alive. The airstrip that they had slaved on for two and a half years had now been rendered virtually unusable due to Allied bombing. Initially, they were forced to repair the airstrip after each attack, but this soon proved impossible, leaving them redundant. With Allied landings expected at any time, the Japanese decided to move two of their battalions to the west coast, near Api, to try to counter the feared Allied invasion. Movement to sea was by now out of the question due to American submarines operating in the Celebes Sea.

Four hundred and seventy of the fittest prisoners left at Sandakan were chosen as carriers. The group was made up of 370 Australians and 100 British.

It was estimated that the 225-mile trek through dense jungle would take three weeks. Such a trek would test the fittest soldiers, let alone weak, sick and starving prisoners burdened with heavy loads, but they had little choice.

A route had been mapped out for the Japanese by the chief of the Dasan tribe, called Kulang, who, being anti-Japanese, deliberately proposed the worst possible course without knowing that prisoners of war would be going along. They were expected to cover around 10 miles a day over rough terrain and through crocodile-infested swamps.

The prisoners, under the command of Captain Yamamoto Shoichi, were split into nine groups of around fifty, with one group departing each day. Before setting off they were given four days' rations, with further food to be collected at specified food dumps en route. They were also given 30 grams of tobacco, a pair of second-hand shorts and shirt, and for any who did not have boots (most of them), a pair of rubber slip-on shoes. They were also allowed to kill several pigs and a horse to take a long as extra food, but this of course added to their burden.

The trek started at 0600 hrs on 29 January, when the first group left Sandakan under the command of Lieutenant Iino Shigeru, with the final group leaving on 6 February. As they set off, they were told much of the supplies to be provided en route would not be available, and that the four-day rations they had been given were to last for eight days. For some reason, this information was not passed on to the later groups, who ate their food within the first four days and many died of starvation.

Keith Botterill, one of the survivors of the march, testified at the war crimes tribunals after the war:

> There were men, about one or two, left behind every second or third day. Of a morning those who were too sick, would tell our Australian officer in charge that they could not move with the party. The Japanese Sergeant or officer would then count the rest of us, and we would move off, after we were half a mile or so along the road, we would hear shots.

> The Japanese officer told us that they had been ordered to shoot the men who were left behind. At times when we were marching along the road, some of the men who were too weak to keep up dropped behind. The Japanese would shoot them. … I can remember going up a big mountain at Boto and we lost five men, I myself saw a Japanese corporal shoot two of them.

When the first of the five groups reached Ranau, a small village in the foothills of Mount Kinabalu, the prisoners were in a very bad state, many suffering from malaria or beriberi. With so many men in such a bad state, the Japanese decided that it was now impossible to continue to Tuaran, and the march was halted. Only 190 out of the original 470 Australian prisoners who set off in the nine groups survived the march. They were immediately set to work, building huts for the Japanese along with a temporary camp for themselves.

One of the men, Gunner Albert Cleary, was so desperate that he tried to escape into the jungle. He was recaptured a week later, beaten up and tied to a log for ten days. During those days, he was beaten, spat at, and urinated on by the Japanese guards. A Japanese officer warned the rest of the prisoners: 'If you try to escape the same thing will happen to you.'

When Cleary was eventually released, close to death, the other prisoners carried him to a stream, washed him, gave him some food, and placed him in a hut, where he died a few days later.

By the end of May, there were only around thirty prisoners left alive at Ranau. Despite the risk, two men, Privates Richard Murray and Keith Botterill, stole rice from the Japanese to build up food stocks for a planned escape. When the theft was discovered, Murray stepped forward to take responsibility, aware he would be killed. He was bayoneted and his body thrown into a bomb crater. Murray sacrificed his life to save his friend, Keith Botterill.

Back in Sandakan, the Japanese ordered 536 out of the 724 remaining prisoners to set off for Ranau once again. Most of these men who had been too ill to undertake the first march were still in a bad way, many suffering from scabies, tropical ulcers, and other diseases. Once again, Japanese cruelty knew no bounds and the debilitated men were forced to load up their meagre belongings and set off marching.

Most of the guards for this march were Taiwanese, and one of them, called Toyoshige Karashima, testified after the war that conditions for the prisoners were dreadful:

> The food situation was terribly bad and a lot of them (the prisoners) were sick. They had malaria and things like that, so they were weak. We were told that if they fell over, we shouldn't leave them lying there. We had to get rid of them. It was maybe three or five days into the march and there had been very heavy rain the night before, so the prisoners were cold and shivering. About thirty of them couldn't keep up, so we gathered them up and dealt with them … the only thing we could do was to get rid of them because they couldn't keep up. The prisoners were put in a kind of valley and so we shot them from above. If they had weapons it would have been different – but it made me think, because I have a conscience. But we were told that we had to follow orders, and if we didn't then we would be killed ourselves. A few days later an Australian prisoner fell, exhausted in the jungle. For an hour I tried to find ways of taking him with me, but I couldn't. He said he wanted to drink coffee and eat bread, but that was impossible. I did have some bread and I'd eaten about half of it, so I gave him the other half. I thought that he might now be able to walk, but he couldn't. He said, 'please kill me' and when I looked at his legs it was very clear that he wouldn't be able to stand up – he wouldn't be able to walk. His thighs were very swollen. He knew that he couldn't do anything and said he was happy to die. He gave me a photograph and address and asked me to send the photograph to the address. I think it was a photograph of his family. After the war we had a very hard time, so I just threw it away. After he had finished his bread, I had no choice but to kill him.
>
> [After the war, Karashima was found guilty of murdering Australian prisoners of war and sent to prison for ten years.]

This second march took almost four weeks, with only 183 of the original 536 reaching Ranau – a horrendous death toll. Many had either died en route or been killed by the Japanese guards because they were too weak to continue.

By this time, the 288 prisoners still left at Sandakan were so ill that the Japanese intended to leave them to die of starvation, but seventy-five were picked out to form another group to make a death march to Ranau, leaving on 10 July, just over a month before the war ended. This group were in a bad state and none of them survived beyond 30 miles. As each man collapsed, the Japanese guards simply bayoneted him. The 213 very ill men who were left at Sandakan were either murdered by the Japanese guards or died of starvation.

As the war drew to close in August 1945, there were only thirty-eight prisoners left alive at Ranau, out of the 373 who had managed to get there. These men were too ill to work so the Japanese officer in charge decided that they should be shot.

When the Japanese surrendered on 15 August, not one of the prisoners who had endured the Sandakan death marches was still alive. Only six men, who had managed to escape into the jungle from the camp at Ranau, survived to tell the tale.

Four of the six, Private Keith Botterill, Bombardier Bill Moxham, Private Nelson Short and Gunner Francis 'Andy' Anderson, made a run for it on 7 July and managed to survive for a few weeks in a local village to the west of Ranau. Three weeks later, Warrant Officer William Sticpewich and his friend Private Herman 'Alby' Reither also managed to escape. Sticpewich managed to survive but unfortunately, Reither died a week later. Sticpewich and Botterill gave evidence at the Tokyo War Crimes Tribunal about the atrocities, giving a full account of what the men went through during that three-year period.

Of the six escapees, three died later and the other three bore witness at the war crimes trials at Rabaul and Tokyo in 1946. Fourteen Japanese officers were convicted of war crimes in Borneo and were executed.

The death toll during the Sandakan marches was horrendous: 1,381 Australian prisoners of war died, along with 641 British and around 4,000 Javanese slave labourers. After the war, very few Japanese officers admitted liability for the atrocities carried out at Sandakan, and all documents relating to the camp and the marches were burned.

The Sandakan death march remains the greatest single atrocity committed against the Australians and British during the Second World War.

Chapter 13
Other Atrocities

Comfort Women

The term 'comfort woman', *'ianfu'* in Japanese, literally means 'comforting, consoling woman' and is a euphemistic way of referring to women forced to provide sexual services for the Japanese military from 1932 to 1945. It was to be the largest case of government-sponsored human trafficking and sexual slavery in modern history.

The official reasons given by the Japanese for setting up a comfort women system were:

1. To prevent the rape of women in territory newly occupied by their military.
2. To prevent the large-scale raping of women by the Japanese military when it expanded its network of influence in China.
3. To prevent the spread of sexually transmitted diseases among the Japanese military forces.

After the Rape of Nanking in 1937 (as outlined in Chapter 2), they enlarged their comfort women programme all over South East Asia. Women from Korea, China, Indonesia, Netherlands, and the Philippines were recruited, with promises of jobs in restaurants and factories, but they were then sent to military brothels where they were forced to service dozens of Japanese soldiers every day. Often on the front line, these women suffered great mental and physical anguish. If any comfort girl was wounded, she would be abandoned or shot to prevent capture.

There were two groups of comfort women. One group was made up of women who were voluntarily recruited and conscripted by the highest levels of the Japanese military. The second group comprised women who were abducted or otherwise conscripted by Japanese military units stationed in occupied territories. The Japanese commanding military officer in a certain area could order the procurement of local women to serve as comfort women. These women were not subjects of Japan but were classified as 'spoils of war'.

When the Japanese invaded the Dutch island of Java (now Indonesia) on 8 March 1942, many of the civilian population were interned in camps where the conditions were atrocious. They were given very little food and were forced to eat snails and rats just to survive.

A young Dutch girl in her late teens called Jan Ruff managed to survive the deprivations of her captivity for two and a half years until September 1944, when Japanese officers entered her camp and ordered all the girls over the age of 17 to line up. Ten girls, including Ruff, were ordered to pack a small suitcase before being loaded into a truck that drove them away. Ruff's initial thoughts were that they were being taken to work in a factory, but this was not to be the case as they were driven to a large house. On arrival, each girl was photographed, given a Japanese name and allocated a room with their photographs pinned up at the entrance. Jan Ruff recalled what happened after the war ended:

> We were forced into trucks. We huddled together like frightened animals and drove through the hillside suburb of Semarang. The truck stopped in front of a large house. Seven girls were told to get out. I was one of them. We were made to understand that we were here for the sexual pleasure of the Japanese. In other words, we found ourselves in a brothel. We were to always obey; we were not allowed to leave the house. In fact, the house was guarded and trying to escape was useless. We were in this house for only one purpose, for the Japanese to have sex with us. We were enslaved into enforced prostitution. We protested loudly that we would never allow this to happen to us, that it was against all human rights, that we would rather die. The Japanese stood there laughing, saying that they were our captors, and they could do with us as they liked, and if we did not obey our families would suffer.
>
> Opening night arrived. We were all terrified and we huddled together in the dining room. We were all virgins and none of us knew anything about sex. We were all so innocent and we tried to find out from each other what to expect and what was going to happen to us. We were ordered to each go to our rooms, but we refused, clinging to each other for safety. My whole body was burning up with fear. It is a feeling I can't

> possibly describe, a feeling I shall never forget and never lose. Even after almost fifty years I still experience this feeling of total fear going through my body and limbs, burning me up. I hid under the dining room table. Eventually I was found and dragged out. A large Japanese officer stood in front of me, looking down at me, grinning at me. I kicked him in the shins. He just stood there laughing. My fighting, kicking, crying, and protesting made no difference. He became extremely angry. He took his sword out of its scabbard and pointed it at me, threatening me with it. He was getting impatient by now and he threw me on the bed. He tore off my clothes and threw himself on top of me, pinning me down under his heavy body. I tried to fight him off, I kicked him, I scratched him, but he was too strong. The tears were streaming down my face as he raped me. I can find no words to describe this most inhuman and brutal rape. To me it was worse than dying. During this time the Japanese stripped me of everything, my self-esteem, my dignity, my possessions, and my family.

The Dutch girls also had to submit to a humiliating physical examination by a male Japanese doctor every week and Japanese soldiers were able to watch these examinations. Jan Ruff was raped by a doctor on every occasion after he examined her.

After three months of serial raping, the ten Dutch girls were taken back to a different camp in Batavia (Jakarta today), where they were kept separate from the other women in the camp. They were threatened that their families would be killed if they told anyone about their experiences. Many of the other women in the camp believed that the ten girls had gone voluntarily as prostitutes for money and food, and called them whores.

When the war ended in August 1945, Jan Ruff had the courage to break her silence to a Catholic priest who visited the camp. Prior to the Japanese invasion, she had wanted to become a nun, but when she told the priest about her experiences, he said that it would not be appropriate for her to become a nun, leaving her feeling dirty and ashamed. His words loomed large over her for the rest of her life.

For the next fifty-seven years, Jan Ruff kept her experiences to herself, until in 1992, she had heard that as many as 200,000 other women had shared their experiences as comfort women and were demanding an apology from the Japanese government. She then bravely decided to tell her own story, joining them in a battle to try to force the Japanese government to make a full and public apology. Jan Ruff was the first European comfort woman to speak out.

After the war ended, the Japanese denied that comfort women were forced into sexual slavery, claiming that they were willing prostitutes who were paid for their work. Historians have estimated that as many as 200,000 women were forcibly conscripted in Japanese-occupied countries between 1931 and 1945, to serve as sexual slaves.

In 1992, Japanese historian Yoshiaki Yoshimi published material based on his research in archives at Japan's National Institute for Defence Studies. He discovered seven official documents suggesting that imperial military forces directly forced women to work in frontline brothels in China, Indochina and Indonesia. In one of the documents, a Japanese lieutenant confesses to having organised a brothel and having used it himself. In another, he discovered that women were arrested in the streets, and after enforced medical examinations, were put into brothels against their will.

Many comfort women died as the war progressed, with some, along with many other Japanese soldiers and civilians, choosing suicide rather than surrender to the Allied forces.

It was not until the 1980s and early '90s, when a few elderly Korean women began to speak about their experience at the hands of the Japanese military, that the Japanese even acknowledged the existence of comfort women and apologised for their treatment. By the late 1990s, the comfort women issue had become front-page news in the United States – an issue that was fronted by the women's rights movement, whose groups demanded that the Japanese government acknowledge their responsibility. Even today, the existence of the comfort women during the Second World War is still disputed in Japan.

Cannibalism, 1942–1945

For many centuries, cannibalism was often perceived as an act of desperation by starving peoples. However, during the 1930s and '40s, the Japanese used cannibalism to terrorise their enemies when they embarked on their greater South East Asia Co-Prosperity Sphere campaign. There is evidence that their soldiers ate the flesh of civilians they had killed in China during the 1930s. One Japanese soldier called Nakao recalled an incident involving one of his comrades at that time:

> He captured a thirty-year-old Chinese man, bayoneted him to death, cut off about 1.5kg of flesh from his thigh, wrapped the flesh in cloth, and brought it to me. After the flesh was fried with pork, chicken, fish, and vegetables, all members of the squad of forty soldiers and I ate the dish.

Another Japanese soldier called Takashi Mikami confessed after the war to harvesting brains from live Chinese captives. He said that he was ordered to do so by a sergeant who had heard that eating human brains could treat venereal disease.

On 18 November 1944, a high-ranking Japanese officer called Major General Aozu issued an order to all Japanese troops that said: 'The consumption of enemy flesh is excluded from the military crime of cannibalism and that any soldiers found eating human flesh other than that of the enemy will be guilty of cannibalism, a crime punishable by execution.' A clear indication to the lower ranks that it was perfectly OK for them to consume the flesh of their enemies.

By late 1944, Japanese forces were coming under severe pressure from Australian troops in Papua New Guinea. With the Allies closing in all over South East Asia, they were left to fend for themselves without supplies of food and ammunition. The American fleet was sinking any Japanese ship that tried to bring supplies to the island. As their situation became desperate, they resorted to cannibalism. One Indian prisoner of war, called Hatam Ali, who was on the island at the time and narrowly escaped, said:

> We were taken to a place 300 miles away and worked twelve hours a day with very little food. Anyone who fell ill were killed. When the Japanese ran out of rations, we were forced to eat grass, leaves, snakes, frogs, and other insects. At this stage the Japanese started selecting prisoners and every day one prisoner was taken out and killed and eaten by the Japanese. I personally saw this happen. Those selected were taken to a hut where flesh was cut from their bodies while they were still alive and they were thrown into a ditch alive, where they later died. When flesh was being cut from those selected terrible cries and shrieks came from them and also from the ditch where they were later thrown. These cries used to gradually dim down when the unfortunate individuals were dying. We were not allowed to go near this ditch, new earth was thrown on their bodies and the smell was terrible.

When it was Ali's turn to be to be killed, he ran away as he was taken towards a hut. He then spent the next two weeks wandering around the jungle before he was rescued by Australian forces.

Also in Papua New Guinea, an Indian army soldier who had defected to the Japanese, called Havildar Chandgi Ram, was appalled at what he saw being carried out by the Japanese. He even wondered if he was dreaming:

> On 12 November 1944, I was digging a trench for the Japanese in the Totabil area of New Britain. About 1600 hrs a single-engine United States fighter plane made a forced landing about a hundred yards away from where I was working. The Japanese belonging to Go Butai Kendebo Camp rushed to the spot and seized the pilot, who could not have been more than twenty years old and had managed to scramble out of the plane before they could reach him. About half an hour from the time of the forced landing, the troops beheaded the pilot. I saw this from behind a tree and watched some of the Japanese cut flesh from his arms, legs, hips and buttocks and carry it off to their quarters. I was so shocked at the scene and followed the Japanese just to find out what they would do with the flesh. They cut it in small pieces and fried it. Later that evening a senior Japanese officer, of the rank of major-general, addressed several of the officers. At the conclusion of his speech a piece of fried flesh was given to all present who ate it on the spot.

Another Indian soldier called Jemadar Abdul Latif, of 4/9 Jat Regiment Indian Army, also witnessed cannibalism. He alleged that it was not just prisoners of war who were eaten, but also local people in Papua New Guinea.

A Captain Pirzai and Subedar Doctor Gurcharan Singh of the Indian Army told the Australian *Courier-Mail* on 25 August 1945:

> Of 300 men who went to Wewak with me, only fifty got out. Nineteen were eaten. A Japanese doctor – Lieutenant Tumisa, formed a party of three or four men and would send an Indian outside the camp for something. They would immediately kill him and eat the flesh from his body. The liver, muscles from the buttocks, thighs, legs, and arms would be cut off and cooked.

Many years after the war, a Japanese veteran called Shoji Ogawa wrote about an incident in Papua New Guinea where he discovered a body in the jungle that had been chopped to pieces. He described the scene:

> We were called by a group of four or five soldiers who were not in our troop. They had just finished a meal and there were mess tins nearby. They said that they had a large cut of snake meat and invited us to join in. It was obvious that it was human flesh. I hurried away.

With the war nearing its end in mid-1945, cannibalism reared its head again in the Philippines. In the Bukidnon Region, when the Suzuki Unit, led by General Ainoda, was beginning to run desperately short of food, they resorted to eating the bodies of people who had been killed in action. At the war crimes tribunals, Ainoda argued that he had to find food for his troops and said: 'Whenever possible, we avoided eating the bodies of people who died from illness or were killed in action or were executed for crimes.'

This statement, however, proved to be false, when another Japanese soldier in the same unit called Rikimi Yamamoto testified:

> We frequently ate human meat as our dinner, boiled it with vegetables and ate it. The meat was brought into camp by patrols who had cut it up and dressed it. Sometimes the meat was dried, and sun cured. Since no other meat was available, we had to eat human flesh. For this reason, Filipinos were captured and butchered. I was so hungry I ate it, although I would have preferred pork.

At the war crimes tribunals, a testimony by a Filipino lieutenant called Alejandro Sale was read out by the prosecutor:

> When Lieutenant Alejandro Sale captured the Suzuki Unit, he found human bones and human flesh in the process of cooking, human skulls and fragments of the human body around the premises of the camp of the Suzuki Unit. Also in and around the houses occupied by the members of the Unit. It can therefore be concluded that the killing of Filipinos and the eating of their flesh were of common knowledge to all the members of the Unit who were encamped together in one place.

An Australian soldier called Bill Spencer came across cannibalism when his unit approached Sananada, Papua New Guinea, in 1944. He recalled:

> It was the first area that we had seen cannibalism, the Japanese had been eating our dead parts ... they cut flesh off the legs and the buttocks of our men, and they had the meat in dixies, and they were cooking it in the pots when we moved through the area, horrible a horrible sight.

A medical orderly in the Philippines called Hiaoka Hisashi summed up the Japanese dilemma near the end of the war when he said:

> I have seen people kill live humans and eat them. When I saw someone eat another human being, I thought it looked delicious ... this was the reality. I'm sure you would never look at the organs of a cat or a dog that had died in an accident and think they look delicious. Well, I did. This is how we humans, in the end, turn into wild animals. I think it was much better to die in battle than die of starvation.

After the war, a Japanese major called Matoba Sueo, said: 'Yes, I was a madman due to the war, and that is the only reason I can give for being a cannibal.'

There have been various reports about Japanese cannibalism that allege they particularly ate the entrails and genitals of their victims. Brains were also taken out and eaten, along with intestines.

It was not just Australian soldiers who were eaten in New Guinea and neighbouring small islands; many cases were reported of cannibalism carried out against Indian, Chinese, and Malaysian prisoners of war and civilians.

At the war crimes tribunals, there were very few prosecutions for cannibalism as many of the people testifying did not actually witness the acts; they had merely seen the results.

Acts of cannibalism remain one of the darker crimes carried out by the Japanese during the war. Written reports and testimonies collected by the Australian War Crimes Section of the Tokyo Tribunal proved without doubt that Japanese personnel in many parts of Asia and the Pacific committed acts of cannibalism against Allied prisoners of war.

Pingdingshan Massacre, 1932

On 16 September 1932, the Japanese Army committed one of their earliest atrocities in the village of Pingdingshan, also known as Eagle City, in central Henan province of China.

A band of Chinese resistance fighters led by Liang Jufu burned down several storehouses run by the Japanese in the village and destroyed a coal mine at Yangbaibao. In revenge, they herded the 3,000 residents of the village, including women and children, into a compound surrounded by barbed wire, and machine-gunned them. Only twenty or thirty survived the massacre. The village was then burned to the ground. One 9-year-old girl who survived, called Yang Yufen, recalled the incident many years later:

> The Japanese soldiers told us they were going to take our picture and gathered us in a group. But under the black cloth they didn't have cameras, they had machine guns. The soldiers even bayoneted bodies to ensure the villagers were dead. I survived because my parents shielded me with their bodies. Eighteen members of my family were massacred.

Shanghai, 1937

On Friday, 13 August 1937, the Japanese launched an attack on the Chinese city of Shanghai. The National Revolutionary Army of the Republic of China tried to defend the city, but the Japanese strength eventually overwhelmed them, and it fell into Japanese hands. Described as 'Stalingrad on the Yangtze', this conflict was to turn out to be one of the bloodiest battles of the Sino–Japanese War and is said by many historians to be the start of the Second World War.

The Japanese had expected to clear Shanghai in a few days, but the elite Chinese divisions fought them to a standstill, inflicting heavy casualties, destroying the Japanese perception of military superiority and Chinese inferiority. As a result, they developed a bitter feeling of resentment, taking out their revenge on the civilian population of the city, going on the rampage, looting, raping, and murdering Chinese troops and innocent civilians.

Allow me to digress here, as just over a year later, in September 1938, my own father arrived at Shanghai with his regiment, the 2 East Surreys, as a peacekeeping force based in the International Settlement. Fearing reprisals from Britain and the USA, the Japanese did not occupy the International Settlement but they did try to dominate it through terrorism and subversive activities. It was part of my father's regiment's task to counter such a threat to the multicultural citizens of Shanghai.

At that time, Shanghai was a city shattered by terrible destruction; it was a truly cosmopolitan but dangerous place, with its lurid vice, savage violence, and conspiratorial atmosphere. As my father gazed across the rooftops, he could see the flattened buildings and burnt-out skyscrapers of a city that was being gradually destroyed.

As an occupying force, the Japanese treated the residents of Shanghai very badly and the East Surrey men found this very frustrating. They were just itching to 'have a go' for such maltreatment, but this was out of the question due to the political situation. Their commanding officer, Colonel Swinton, made several formal complaints to the Japanese municipal authorities about the treatment of the local people, but to no avail.

By the summer of 1940, the situation in Shanghai was becoming even tenser. Japanese sabre-rattling had increased considerably, and the population continued to be subjected to terrible atrocities daily. My father told me: 'We just wanted to get out there and kick the shit out of the little bastards.'

With the increased threat from the Japanese, British troops were withdrawn from Shanghai in August 1940. My father's regiment, the East Surreys, were shipped out to Hong Kong.

A letter from a Japanese soldier who wrote home from Shanghai at the time was published after the war:

> During my time at the front in China about the only two things I have learnt are rape and robbery … the looting by our armies is beyond imagination, the prisoners taken from the Chinese army were sometimes lined up in a line and shot just to give us practice in machine-gun traversing fire.

Another Japanese soldier wrote:

> After we had captured a family of four, we played with the daughter as we would a harlot. As the parents kept insisting that their daughter should be returned to them, we killed the father and mother. We then

played with the daughter again as before, until our unit marched on, when we killed her.

Such letters sent home without censorship indicates that the Japanese high command was aware of the atrocities going on in Shanghai during their occupation of the city.

Quzhou Massacre, 1940

On 4 October 1940, a Japanese aircraft flew over the towns of Ningbo and Quzhou in the Chinese province of Western Zhejiang, dropping plague-infected fleas as well as introducing plague-infested rats. Over the next few days, many people in the town and surrounding district died. A 12-year-old boy called Wu Tufu remembered the aircraft coming over as it flew very low, dropping fleas and grains over the streets. Over 2,000 people died in the area during the following twelve months, and indeed, people were to die from disease right up until 1948. (The idea to disseminate plague-infected fleas with grains on Chinese communities came from Unit 731, as mentioned in Chapter 1.)

A 9-year-old boy from Quzhou called Qiu Mingxuan, who lost some of his friends and family to the plague, decided to become a doctor when he left school. After gaining a degree in epidemiology, he returned to the town, determined to find out the truth about the plague epidemic.

At a war crimes trial in Tokyo, Qiu Mingxuan was able to prove that before the Japanese attack, no cases of plague had ever been reported in the area but he couldn't produce enough evidence to prove that it had been started by infected fleas dropped from Japanese aircraft.

Murder on Wake Island, December 1941

Four days after they bombed Pearl Harbor on 7 December 1941, the Japanese invaded Wake Island, a small atoll some 2,458 miles west of Hawaii. Stationed on the island were around 1,187 US marines and over 1,000 civilian workers, mainly contractors employed by the Morrison-Knudsen Company.

They quickly overran the defenders but suffered over 500 casualties in the process. The island fell two days before Christmas.

Furious at losing so many men, the victorious Japanese troops forced the American marines to sit naked on a concrete runway in the blazing sun, their hands tied behind their backs and shackled to their necks. They were made to sit there without food or water for three days. When the Japanese set up machine guns around the perimeter, the men were convinced they would be shot. One American marine said: 'They stripped us down balls and ass naked and hog tied us.'

At the end of the third day, the Japanese commander, Rear Admiral Shigematsu Sakaibara, via an interpreter, told the prisoners: 'The Emperor has graciously presented you with your lives.' One American soldier shouted out, 'Well, thank the son of a bitch for me.'

Tensions of the previous three days relaxed a bit, and they were allowed to retrieve clothing, food and tobacco from their dugouts. They were allowed to bury their dead and were fed well for the first time, before being marched to the north end of the island and put into the barracks they had used before the beginning of hostilities. Several forty-man barracks were packed with 150 men each, but the men had shelter at last.

Most of the men were soon to be shipped to Japan on the *Nitta Maru* (see Chapter 10) whilst 350 civilian contractors were kept because of their skills in operating heavy equipment. They would continue to assist the Japanese military build-up of Wake Island with the same supplies and equipment that they had used for the US Navy. For the next two years, these men would labour under very difficult conditions for their captors.

Towards the end of 1943, the Japanese became convinced that the American civilian contractors remaining on Wake Island were making radio contact with US forces and reporting Japanese positions. Sakaibara ordered the execution of ninety-six men he suspected of doing this. The men were marched to a beach, where they were machine-gunned and buried in a mass grave.

An account of this atrocity may not ever have surfaced had it not been for Lieutenant Commander Tachibana, of the Imperial Japanese Army, who had been on the island at the time. He testified to the war crimes tribunals:

> On 7 October, just after sundown, I don't remember the time, the commanding officer Rear-Admiral Sakibaira and I were at the command post. Then, suddenly, he gave the order that the headquarters company leader is to use his men and shoot to death the prisoners of war on the northern shore. It was so sudden that I was startled, but I knew that

the CO was a careful man and that he wouldn't come to a conclusion unless he had given it plenty of consideration. I didn't, therefore, have any doubt and thought it was justifiable to execute all the prisoners of war according to the situation that night. At 1730 hrs that very afternoon a new officer, named Lieutenant Ito, had just arrived from Kwajalein by plane to take over command of the headquarters company and shortly after his arrival the CO's order was passed on to him by Lieutenant-Commander Tachibana. When Lieutenant Ito arrived at the beach where the massacre was to take place, he saw the prisoners – there were ninety-six of them, sitting side by side in one rank with their backs to the sea. They had been blindfolded and their hands were bound behind their backs. Behind them stood the firing squad. A platoon commander reported that everything was ready and was told by the company commander to go ahead as ordered. When the prisoners had been shot Lieutenant Ito returned to the command post to report.

Atrocities on Guam, December 1941

Three days after their attack on Pearl Harbor, on 7 December 1941, the Japanese invaded the island of Guam, the southernmost part of the Mariana Islands in the Pacific Ocean. It was the first United States-controlled territory to be conquered during the Second World War. When they declared war on Japan, the United States government were aware that it would be difficult to defend Guam if it was attacked by the Japanese. There was only a small US Navy force as well as an Insular Force Guard amounting to around 514 men, on the island.

In the early morning of 10 December, the Japanese South Seas Detachment, a unit of about 5,500 army troops under the command of Major General Tomitarō Hori, and a special navy land force of about 400 men led by Commander Hiroshi Hayashi and drawn from the 5th Defence Force stationed in Saipan, landed on Guam. A few skirmishes took place across the island, before the governor, George McMillin, had no choice but to surrender.

Over the following few weeks, the Japanese flooded the island with around 14,000 army and navy personnel, taking over all government buildings and many private homes. Guam's population, mainly made up of Chamorros, the indigenous people of the Mariana Islands, with the rest being Filipinos, were subjected to a dawn-to-dusk curfew and had their cars, radios and cameras confiscated. They were required to obtain passes – a piece of cloth with Japanese characters – to move about the island.

Many of the Insular Force Guard were interrogated and beaten during the first few weeks of the occupation, suspected of hiding machine guns or other weapons.

Out of six US Navy seamen who had evaded capture, five were caught by the Japanese and beheaded. The only survivor was a radio operator called George Ray Tweed, who was helped by the local Chamorros, moving him from village to village, sometimes endangering their own families for his protection. Several of the Chamorros were questioned, tortured, and beheaded. Tweed managed to evade the Japanese during their occupation of Guam for two years and seven months until he was rescued.

For the next three years, the people of Guam were to suffer greatly at the hands of the Japanese.

On 15 July 1944, as the war neared its end, thirty young Chamorro men and women were taken to caves near Fena Lake. The Japanese murdered fifteen of them using grenades and bayonets; the other fifteen, though badly injured, managed to survive by feigning death.

As American bombing of the island became more intense during late 1944, the Japanese began to move more young people, mostly aged between 16 and 19, into the caves in the Fena area. They were given whiskey and sake to drink as a reward for their hard work helping the occupying forces, but as they were celebrating, the Japanese soldiers machine-gunned them. A group of around twelve young women were forced into a cave and raped by Japanese soldiers, before being beheaded.

In July 1944, a week before American forces landed on Guam, forty men and women in Merizo (now Malesso) were forced into two caves called Tinta and Faha, located on the outskirts of the village. Sixteen were killed before a severe rainstorm prevented them all being killed. Three youngsters who were out in the jungle looking for food in Yona were tied to coconut trees and beheaded. Seven young girls were taken by a Japanese officer into a cave, where he gave them food and sake before raping them.

Towards the end of the war, the local population became so incensed about the massacres and the rapes that they decided to attack the Japanese in revenge. Twenty young men stormed the Japanese quarters, grabbing whatever weapons they could lay their hands on, before killing every soldier in sight.

When the US forces moved onto Guam on 21 July 1944, the Japanese garrison fought practically to the last man. American casualties included 1,700 dead and 6,000 wounded, with Japanese deaths totalling 18,000. Some small units fought on until after the end of the war, causing occasional US casualties, and one solitary veteran only emerged from the jungle to surrender and return to Japan in 1972.

The American troops were horrified to discover many of the mutilated and beheaded bodies of the local population. More than 1,100 Chamorros are estimated to have died during the Japanese occupation, with around 14,704 surviving.

The Tol Plantation Atrocities, Papua New Guinea, January 1942

On the morning of 23 January 1942, the Japanese landed around 20,000 troops at Rabaul in the province of New Britain, Papua New Guinea. New Britain, the largest island in the Bismarck Archipelago, was under Australian rule and defended by 1,396 men of the Australian 2/22 Battalion of the 8th Division, AIF, the New Guinea Volunteer Rifles, and men of the 2/10 Field Ambulance Unit.

With very little chance of defeating the Japanese, soldiers and civilians fled all over the island looking for escape routes through the rugged terrain. Some, despite battling malaria, dysentery, tropical ulcers, leeches, exhaustion, malnutrition, and crocodile-infested rivers, eventually managed to escape in small boats. Some special service units managed to escape into the jungles with the aim of conducting guerrilla warfare on the invading Japanese forces.

The troops that didn't manage to get away were rounded up by the Japanese, tied together with ropes in groups of ten or twelve and taken into the jungle, where they were shot or bayoneted. Some of the Australian soldiers prayed and begged for their lives whilst others said goodbye to their friends; even requests for final cigarettes were refused. Several managed to survive by feigning death and were able to tell their stories after the war. One of them, Private Billy Cook of the 2/12 Field Ambulance, survived eleven bayonet wounds, he recalled:

> They marched us to a plantation about half a mile beyond Tol in the direction of Rabaul. We were ordered, by signs, to sit down on a slight

> rise on the track which led from the road to the plantation. They then began to take the men down the track in twos and threes. I was in the last party which numbered three. The officer, still using signs, asked whether we would rather be bayoneted or shot. We chose the latter. When we reached the end of the track, three Japanese with fixed bayonets took us over and walked on behind us. All three in my group were then knocked to the ground, and as our hands were bound behind our backs and we were also tied together we were unable to move. They bayoneted us several times. I received five bayonet wounds, but I held my breath and feigned death though still alive. As the Japanese were moving off the man next to me groaned. One of the Japanese soldiers came running back and stabbed him once more. By this time, I could hold my breath no longer. When I drew a deep breath, the soldier heard me and inflicted six more bayonet wounds. The last thrust went through my ear into my mouth severing an artery on the way. The member of the escort seeing the blood gushing out of my mouth assumed that I was at last dead, covered the three of us with coconut fronds and vine leaves and left. I lay there for approximately one hour, then I decided to try and get away. I managed to undo the cord which bound me to the other two and started to walk towards the sea, which was only fifty yards away. After taking a few steps I collapsed. It seemed only a short time before I regained consciousness. I then tried to saw through the bonds round my hands with the iron heel of my boot, but without success. Eventually I managed aged to get my leg between my two hands and, raising it, chewed at the cord until it came apart.

Cook managed to escape into the jungle – as did five other survivors – who were eventually evacuated from New Britain to Port Moresby along with 156 soldiers, sailors and civilians, aboard the overcrowded government yacht *Laurabada*.

The civilian population of Rabaul also suffered at the hands of the Japanese invaders. Drunken soldiers went from house to house, raping, looting, and killing, particularly in the Chinatown district. An 11-year-old Australian boy called Dickie Manson was living with his mother Marjorie and his father Ted just outside the city, where they owned a plantation. The family decided to flee into the jungle, but before they could manage to get away, they were betrayed by one of the locals, caught and searched by the

Japanese. Ted Manson had a two-way radio with him, and Marjorie had a pistol hidden in her bag. After being tried for espionage, they were found guilty and taken to the base of Tavurvur volcano in the back of an open truck, where they were lined up and shot on the orders of a Japanese naval officer called Mizusaki Shojiro. Eleven-year-old Dicky managed to punch one soldier in the head before he was shot.

At the Japanese headquarters in Waga Waga, near Milne Bay, further atrocities were committed on the Australian troops by the Japanese. A Captain Kendall, who found bodies, said in an affidavit after the war:

> On the track leading from Waga Waga I saw the body of an Australian soldier with his hands tied behind his back, lying face downwards. He was tied with string. He had a wound on his leg with a field dressing on it and had the top of his head cut right off. The top portion of the skull was lying forward as if it had been cut through with a heavy knife or sword and had been chopped from the rear. He also had lacerations criss-crossing his back and shoulders. They appeared to be knife or sword wounds and had cut right through the shirt into his flesh.

In mid-September 1943, several men of an Australian special services unit who were waging a guerrilla war on the Japanese were captured, interrogated, and tortured for two weeks. They were then marched to a beach, blindfolded, and beheaded before being buried in a mass grave. A photograph of one of the men, called Siffleet, being beheaded was found by American troops in 1944. (See illustrations.)

Describing Siffleet's execution, an anonymous Japanese soldier wrote:

> Major Komai stands up and says to the prisoner, 'We are going to kill you.' When he tells the prisoner that in accordance with Japanese 'Bushido' he would be killed with a Japanese sword and would have two- or three-minutes grace, he listens with bowed head. Now the time has come, and the prisoner is made to kneel on the bank of a bomb crater, filled with water. He is apparently resigned. The precaution is taken of surrounding him with guards with fixed bayonets, but he remains calm. He even stretches his neck out. He is a very brave man indeed … The Major had drawn his favourite sword … He taps the prisoner's neck slightly with the back of the blade, then raises above his head with both

> arms and brings it down with a powerful sweep. A hissing sound – it must be the sound of spurting blood, spurting from the arteries: the body falls forward. It is amazing – he has killed him with one stroke. The onlookers crowd forward. The head, detached from the trunk, rolls forward in front of it. The dark blood gushes. It is all over. The head is dead white, like a doll ... A seaman ... turns the headless body over on its back and cuts the abdomen open with one clean stroke.
>
> (From *Eyewitness to History*, Avon Books, 1987)

As the war drew to a close in 1945, Japanese forces in Papua New Guinea were coming under severe pressure from the Australians. Supplies of food and ammunition had run out, and with their situation becoming desperate, they resorted to cannibalism. One Indian prisoner of war on the island said:

> The Japanese started selecting prisoners, and every day one prisoner was taken out and killed and eaten by the soldiers. I personally saw this happen and about 100 prisoners were eaten at this place by the Japanese. Those selected were taken to a hut where their flesh was cut from their bodies while they were alive, and they were thrown into a ditch where they later died.

Another said: 'Japanese soldiers on the island killed and ate about one prisoner per day over the course of 100 days.'

The 3rd Battalion of the 144th Infantry Regiment, commanded by Colonel Masao Kusunose, was the Japanese Army unit responsible for the murders on Papua New Guinea. On 17 December 1946, Kusunose committed suicide by starving himself to death.

The Parit Sulong Massacre, January 1942

By third week of January 1942, the Japanese had pushed the Allied forces down Malaya as far as the small town of Parit Sulong, 100 miles north of Singapore. A few days earlier, Australian soldiers from 2/30th Battalion, assigned to the 27th Brigade of the 8th Division, ambushed Japanese forces near Gemas, some 70 miles further north, and killed or wounded around 1,000 troops of the Japanese 5th Division in a fierce ambush.

The Australian 8th Division and the 45th Indian Infantry Brigade were making fighting withdrawals when they were surrounded near a bridge over the Sungai Simpang-kiri River, just north of Batu Pahat. The Australians and the Indians fought doggedly for two days, and when they began to run low on ammunition and food, their officers ordered them to disperse into the jungle and make their way back towards Allied lines any way they could. Many got away, but approximately 150 Australian and Indian soldiers were too seriously injured to move, and under the command of Captain Rewi Snelling, were left to surrender.

The Japanese were so incensed at their losses at Gemas that the Japanese officer in charge, Lieutenant General Takuma Nishimura, gave the following order to his junior officers: 'Execute all the prisoners by firing squad and kill them. All the bodies of the prisoners ought to be cremated on completion of the execution and all traces of their disposal obliterated.'

On the afternoon of 22 January, the prisoners were beaten and kicked by their captors, before being tied up with wire, petrol poured over them and set alight. Their bodies were then driven over by trucks. Local Malays reported that they saw others being tied together with wire, forced to stand on a bridge and shot, their bodies falling into the river.

Only three men survived the massacre at Parit Sulong; one of them, Ben Hackney, played dead despite being bayoneted eight times. Hackney suffered flashbacks for the rest of his life. His niece, Iris Sheridan, said: 'His memories of his murdered mates were so awful that he never talked about them. He was a generous, caring man but he had moods. He would be pleased the story is finally being told.'

Another one of the three survivors, 18-year-old Jimmy Wharton, was superficially wounded and fell on top of his mate who was more badly injured, groaning and writhing in agony. The Japanese pushed Wharton off his body and into a storm drain, thinking he was dead, before proceeding to finish off his mate with a burst of machine-gun fire. He spent several hours lying motionless in the storm drain, listening in horror to the screams and shouts as the men were set alight, lorries then driven back and forward over their bodies. After the Japanese left, and weak from loss of blood from where a bullet had passed right through his chest, somehow missing his lungs, Wharton crawled into the Malayan darkness. For almost a week, he wandered in a daze through the jungle, before eventually being captured by the Japanese and taken to Pudo Jail in Kuala Lumpur.

One of the Japanese officers involved in the massacre at Parit Sulong, Major Fukashi Hinokunia, had a grim story to tell the War Crimes Commission after the war:

> One hour before dark the prisoners were ordered to make their way to an assembly point at the rear of a row of damage shops. Those who were unable to walk were carried by the walking wounded, while others, also walking wounded, were made to carry the bodies of their dead comrades who were lying in the dust. The pretext used to entice the Indian and Australian prisoners to drag themselves to what was to be a designated execution site, was that medical treatment and food would be provided. Concealed within the rear rooms of damaged shops, three squads of executioners waited behind tripod mounted heavy machine guns. When all the prisoners had arrived at the assembly point and were either sitting or lying prone, depending on the seriousness of their wounds, the machine guns began their wicket thumping chatter of death. Such concentrated machine gun-fire cuts swathes of carnage from three different points, enfilading the closely grouped prisoners, chopping fresh flesh and limbs to pieces. When cries of pain and shock were silenced, so were the machine guns. Seven prisoners had to be bayoneted despite the concentrated gunfire as they still showed signs of life. Funeral pyres were quickly expedited per the simple method of collapsing six abandoned shops with mortars and hand grenades. Following which 161 bodies were carried in an endless stream to the tinder-dry debris and placed in piles where engulfing flames would consume them most efficiently. A considerable amount of paraffin obtained from captured lorries, 40-gallon drums and some 60 gallons of gasoline were then splashed and spilled over and around the corpses. To ensure total incineration, tyres and demolition material from the walls and verandas of the collapsed building were also heaped onto the large pyres.
>
> At 2000 hrs, Morioka give the signal for everyone to stand well clear. Then a flaming torch was thrown. The demolished buildings erupted with a wishing cataclysmic roar. In the event, four adjacent dwellings and nine shops burned to the ground before midnight. The stench of roasting flesh permeated the warm air until the small hours of the morning when the fierce flames had reduced to mere flickers above piles

> of grey, white ash. But even then, radiated heat from concealed red-hot embers could be felt twenty yards away. Without any doubt, the mass cremation like the execution, was an outstanding example of efficiency.

Lieutenant General Nishimura was later found guilty of the Parit Sulong Massacre before an Australian Military Court and sentenced to life imprisonment. After serving four years, he was transferred to Tokyo to serve the rest of his sentence, but when the ship he was travelling on stopped temporarily in Hong Kong, he was seized by the Australian military police and taken to Manus Island, where he was hanged on 11 June 1951.

The Ambon Island Atrocity, February 1942

Located in the Banda Sea, just south of the larger island of Ceram between Indonesia and Papua New Guinea, the Dutch island of Ambon was considered a strategic location by the Allies in the event of a Japanese invasion of Australia. It was an important air and sea link between Australia, New Guinea and the northern Dutch East Indies.

As it was only 800 miles from Darwin, the Australian government understood it could be used by the Japanese as a base from which to launch raids on northern Australia.

On 14 December 1941, the Australian high command sent a convoy carrying over 1,000 troops to reinforce the Dutch forces on Ambon. The convoy arrived at Ambon on 17 December, with further reinforcements arriving a month later.

From 6 January 1942, Ambon was attacked daily by Japanese aircraft, soon rendering the naval aviation base at Halong unusable. By the beginning of February, the Australians and Dutch had surrendered to the Japanese. Many of the troops tried to escape the clutches of the Japanese invaders, two groups managing to escape home to Australia by island-hopping across the Arafura Sea. The rest were captured and taken to the Dutch barracks at Tantui, just north of Ambon town.

Three hundred Australian and Dutch prisoners were murdered near Laha airfield in revenge for the sinking of a Japanese minesweeper. They were led to the site with their arms tied behind their backs, forced to kneel around circular graves about 3 yards apart, and beheaded. The first man was beheaded by a warrant officer called Kakutaro Sasaki. Details of this atrocity were revealed at the end of the war when a Japanese interpreter called Suburo Yoshizaki, was interrogated. He stated:

> Just prior to the commencement of the executions, a Japanese marine (rank and name unknown) came over to where me and my companions were standing and requested the loan of my sword. I loaned his sword to the marine whereupon he disappeared among a group of marines standing about hole 'B'.
>
> The execution of the first Australian prisoner at grave 'A'; this decapitation was carried out by Warrant Officer Kakutaro Sasaki. After the fourth prisoner had been beheaded by individual marines keenly waiting their turn (ranks and names unknown) at grave 'A', several battery torches were procured to light the backs of the necks of each successive victim. After the seventh or eighth Australian had been decapitated at grave 'A', the marine who had borrowed the sword, returned it to me commenting that it was blunt, and the blade had unaccountably bent when he had beheaded a giant of a fellow.
>
> On receipt of my sword and scabbard, I and my companions departed the scene of the killings and returned to our barracks. I did not witness the executions of prisoners at grave 'B' as my attention was concentrated on the macabre drama at grave 'A'. I learned later that in addition to Dutch mortar unit personnel (about thirty prisoners), fifty-five Australian soldiers had also been beheaded on the night in question.

Yoshizaki went on to say:

> On my return to Ambon township on 23 February 1942 (I had been absent on interpreting duties at Paso) I heard from, I believe, 1st Class Petty Officer Tasuki Yamashita that between 15–20th February 1942 (exact date I can't recall) all the remaining prisoners (Australian) at Laha Airfield had been decapitated, some eighty odd as related to me by Yamashita. I was told that this second execution at Laha had been carried out by crew members of a Japanese minesweeper that had been sunk previously by an enemy mine in Ambon Bay. It was an act of reprisal and retaliation for the loss of their ship.

When the war ended, 60 per cent of the Australians and Dutch captured on Ambon were dead.

Murder at Balikpapan, February 1942

During the night of 23 January 1942, Japanese units landed at Balikpapan, a seaport city in East Kalimantan on the east coast of the Dutch island of Borneo. The area contained several oilfields that the Japanese were keen to preserve intact. They were concerned that the oilfields would be destroyed, like those at Tarakan some weeks earlier.

Two Dutch officers, who had been captured at Tarakan at that time, were taken to Balikpapan where they were forced to deliver an ultimatum to the Dutch commanding officer, Lieutenant Colonel Van Den Hoogenband, whereby that if the vital oil installations there were destroyed, all Dutch personnel in the area would be shot. This ultimatum read:

> When the Balikpapan garrison destroys the natural resources and oil-installations at Balikpapan and the surrounding country, all commanding officers, their Dutch soldiers, and other Dutchmen related to them will be killed without exception. Captain Coren and Captain Renduruhof are sent to provide detailed instructions.

Van Den Hoogenband promptly ignored the ultimatum and ordered the oil fields to be destroyed before he escaped with what was left of his group. The Japanese were outraged when they discovered that all the oilfields had been completely destroyed. They rounded up every Dutchmen they could find: two civil servants, a police inspector, a medical officer, eight patients from Balikpapan hospital, three priests and a group of POWs, members of the Royal Dutch East Indies Army, seventy-eight people in all. The group were taken to a beach, where they were forced into the sea and shot. The Japanese brought many of the native Indonesians from neighbouring villages to witness the executions as a reminder as to what might happen if they did not go along with their forces.

One Dutch survivor, Josepa van Amstel, who managed to disguise himself as a native islander, told the war crimes tribunal:

> I could see the Europeans already being lined up. At a distance of about 50 meters, I could recognize Doctor Arps, Doctor Dikstaal, the priest Creutzberg and some of the patients from Balikpapan hospital. While we were forced to watch, the Japanese first beheaded the two

> civil servants (Binnenlands Bestuur) and then chased the others into the sea. They were shot one by one, their bodies drifting in the water. The old priest Creutzberg first tried to talk to the Japanese, hoping to stop the killing, but when that didn't help, he started to bless the victims until he was shot himself.

There is some confusion about the date that this atrocity took place. Some sources state that it happened on 24 February, but others indicate that it was on the 20th.

The Selerang Barracks Singapore Killings, August 1942

One of the atrocities committed by the Japanese in Singapore that is particularly close to my heart concerns the execution of one of my father's fellow soldiers in the East Surrey Regiment – a man called Harold Waters, from Birmingham.

After languishing in Changi with the rest of the surviving East Surreys for seven months, Private Waters, along with three other men, called Gale, Breavington and Fletcher, attempted to escape. They were quickly recaptured and locked up in solitary confinement.

The Japanese were now becoming so concerned about the number of prisoners who were attempting to escape, that Lieutenant General Fukuei Shimpei, the new commander of prisoners in Singapore, demanded that they sign a document undertaking not to escape. When almost everyone in Changi refused to sign, Shimpei was so enraged that he ordered all the prisoners to march to Selerang Barracks in Singapore city. A barracks that was built to house 800 was now crammed with over 17,000 men.

The Japanese reduced the water supply, leaving only one tap for drinking water and none at all for the toilets, resulting in many cases of dysentery breaking out. Living conditions were dreadful, but the men still refused to sign the document. Shimpei then decided that an example should be set, with Waters, Gale, Breavington and Fletcher sentenced to death for attempting to escape. Colonel E.B. Holmes, commanding British and Australian troops at Changi, protested vehemently and drew up a plea for leniency, which was dismissed.

At around midday on 2 September, the four men were driven in a truck to Changi beach to meet their fate. Waters, still in his pyjamas, was in such a bad way from the severe beatings he had been given that he could not walk or stand upright, whilst Breavington was so weak from starvation and beriberi that he had to walk with a stick.

A firing party, made up of Sikh soldiers who had defected to the Japanese, lined them up facing four graves. The British and Australian officers pleaded for the men to be spared, but Shimpei was adamant they were to be shot to set an example for the rest of the prisoners. After a padre had said prayers for the condemned men, each was given a cigarette. The officers saluted the men who bravely returned it before being offered blindfolds, which all four refused.

It was around 1600 hrs when a lieutenant called Okusaki ordered the squad to open fire. The four men, still alive after the first volley of shots, were screaming out in agony before they were finally finished off with a second volley. Bugler Arthur Lane of the Manchester Regiment, who had been the official bugler in Changi since the capitulation, was then called upon to play the Last Post at the execution of the four men. I had the good fortune to visit Arthur at his home near me in Stockport before he passed away, and he vividly recalled that fateful day when the group were executed on Changi beach:

> When we arrived at the scene a large group of Japanese soldiers were already waiting for the carnival to commence. A truck arrived, the back was dropped, and the prisoners were ordered to get down. One of the prisoners [Waters] was wearing his pyjamas, having been brought from the hospital. He could not walk or even stand on his own, so he was assisted by the Padre and one of the officers. The prisoners' names and army details were read out parrot fashion. The three able men were taken to a position where five pieces of wood were protruding from the ground. Each one was placed in position in front of each pole and secured by rope. The fourth man (Waters) was carried to sit upright. There was a preamble in Japanese read out loud, which I believe was the sentence of death, followed by two Japanese officers performing some form of salute using swords. There was a great deal of muttering coming from the English-speaking witnesses, with Colonel Wild stating that the men had not received a fair trial. Whilst this was going on, ten of the defecting Sikhs were marched in line facing the prisoners. A Japanese officer shouted orders at which the ten soldiers lifted their

> rifles to the firing position. On the order to fire they opened up and all three men slumped forward to meet their maker. Our own officers started shouting and swearing at the Japanese, who at gunpoint then ordered them to fall back. The Padre started to pray for the men, and I was ordered to sound the 'Last Post'. I could not do it justice as I was so upset from what I had seen. I was trying not to show my tears and after a feeble attempt at the 'Last Post' the colonel ordered me to follow him.

After the war, Lieutenant Okusaki, the officer in charge of the execution, was captured by a group of Australian soldiers who took him back to Changi beach and, without trial, executed him in retribution. Lieutenant General Fukuei Shimpei was also tried for both forcing the 17,000 men to sign the pledge and forcing them to be confined in the parade square. He also was tried for the execution of the four recaptured prisoners, was found guilty and sentenced to death by shooting. He was shot on the same Changi beach by volunteers of the Northamptonshire Regiment, on 27 April 1946.

A poem was later written by an unknown friend of one of the men, Rodney Breavington, in honour of his courage that day:

> They murdered him in hatred,
> prolonged his tortured end,
> in spite of all his pleadings,
> they turned and shot his friend,
> they said he was an example,
> of what they had in store,
> for others who attempted escape,
> whilst prisoners of war

Massacres on the Andaman Islands, 1942–1945

On 23 March 1942, Japanese forces landed in the Andaman Islands, a group of islands administered by the British, situated in the Bay of Bengal some 400 miles west of Thailand, in the Andaman Sea.

After meeting no resistance, they ran rampage in the villages, raping women and young girls and sodomising young boys. In the capital Port Blair, eight high-ranking Indian officials were tortured before being buried in pits that they themselves had been forced to dig, with only their heads protruding above the ground. Their skulls and eyes were then punctured with bayonets, after which they were all shot.

Other government officials were locked up in the town's gaol, where they were subjected to water treatment, electric shocks, and other dreadful forms of torture. Anyone left alive was taken out into the countryside and murdered.

One of the saddest stories to come out of the atrocities carried out in Port Blair was of a young boy called Zulfikar Ali. When the Japanese first entered the town, Ali picked up a gun and fired it into the air before running away and hiding in a house. The next day, a Japanese officer told the leader of the town, Doctor Diwan Singh Kalepani, that if the boy was not produced, the people would have their homes burned down. Kalepani had no choice but to produce the boy and take him to the Japanese, where he was dragged in front of the people. They proceeded to kick and beat him until he was unconscious, before using him as bayonet practice. For the next nine months, the people of the Andaman Islands lived in fear of Japanese reprisals for any small act of disobedience or any sort of espionage.

As happened in most countries invaded by the Japanese, they shipped Korean comfort girls onto the Andaman Islands. Doctor Singh was ordered to vacate the Gurdwara hospital building so that it could be used as a brothel. The medicines and drugs were confiscated, to be reserved for the Japanese and the comfort girls. When he refused, the hospital was taken by force.

Doctor Singh was also accused of spying, and on 23 October, he was arrested and imprisoned. For two months he was abused, beaten and tortured, hung by his hair from the ceiling, water poured into his mouth and nose, and his bones crushed. He was subjected to electric shocks, fires were lit under his legs, and his eyes were gouged out, before he died in Port Blair on 14 January 1944. This was one of the most horrific tortures carried out during the entire war.

Japanese atrocities on the Andamans continued well into 1944. On 30 January, forty-four members of the Indian Independence League were taken from their prison and driven in trucks to Homfreyganj, where they were shot by a Japanese firing squad, their bodies buried in a mass grave.

In June 1945, with the end of the war in sight, well over 1,000 Andamanese civilians were put on a Japanese aircraft at Port Blair for an unknown destination. As the aircraft flew low over Havelock Island just 50 miles away, they were forced to jump into the sea. Some of them managed to swim ashore, but within a couple of weeks they had all died of hunger, except for one man called Mohammad Saudagar, who survived to tell the story.

Another group of Andamanese were taken to Tarmugli Island, where they were tied to trees and used as bayonet practice, before being incinerated.

In August 1945, with the end of the war only few days away, 300 Andamanese inhabitants were loaded onto boats and taken to an uninhabited island. When the boats were about 100 yards from the beach, they were all forced over the side and left to their fate. Over 100 drowned, with those who made it to the beach left to starve; only eleven survived.

Out of the total population of around 40,000 in Port Blair when the Japanese invaded, 30,000 Andamanese people were murdered. These small islands were left in a scene of utter devastation when the war eventually ended.

The Pig Basket Atrocity, October 1942

When the Japanese invaded the Dutch-controlled island of Java in early March 1942, around 200 Dutch and Australian soldiers took to the hills around the town of Malang. They formed themselves into groups of resistance fighters to strike back at the Japanese, but despite their heroic efforts against a superior force, they were eventually captured and taken prisoner.

The Japanese, with their usual ruthlessness, crammed the soldiers into 3-foot-long bamboo pig baskets and loaded them into trucks three and four high. In each basket was a man who had his hands tied behind his back, legs drawn up and tied to his body with thick ropes. The trucks were then driven under an intense sun to the coast, where they were loaded onto boats and taken out into the shark-infested waters, where they were thrown overboard.

An eyewitness to the men being driven in the trucks was a 15-year-old Dutch girl, Elizabeth Van Kampen. Elizabeth was walking home with her father from his plantation when they clearly saw the trucks drive towards the sea. They heard the prisoners screaming for help and water. She gave this account of the atrocity to me in 2014, when I was writing her book *Two Years of Tenko : Life as a 16-year-old in a Japanese Prisoner of War Camp*.

> One day towards the end of October 1942, as my father and I were walking back home down the main road from the plantation for lunch, we heard the sound of vehicles. As the vehicles were coming towards us, we scrambled off the road and hid behind some bushes where we

watched five trucks come round the bend. As they passed by a matter of yards from us, we were both stunned by the sights and sounds emanating from them. The trucks were piled high with bamboo pig baskets containing not pigs but crammed with screaming men. 'Water, water, please,' they screamed in Dutch and English. My father said softly to me, 'Oh my god, those poor men.' After they had passed, we walked home without saying a word to each other. It was as though we had just emerged from a nightmare. Even today, I can still hear those poor men crying and screaming for help and for water. Over lunch, my father told my mother the whole story. She was also stunned and revolted and could hardly believe that human beings could do such things to each other.

The commander in chief of Japanese forces in Java, General Imamura, was later acquitted of this atrocity in a Netherlands court for lack of evidence, but a subsequent Australian Military Court found him responsible and handed down a sentence of ten years' imprisonment. At least some justice for the horrible sights my father and I witnessed that day.

Another Dutch lady, a Mrs L.M.C., also witnessed the lead-up to the atrocity and gave the following evidence at an enquiry after the war:

> In the second half of April or early May 1943, I was on my way to an estate near Dampit when I saw trucks coming out of a side road and turning on to the main road in my direction. This road is only five to six metres wide and the driver of my carriage stopped on the end of the road to let the trucks pass. From a distance of about two metres, I saw that four trucks were loaded with baskets, stacked three and four high. In each basket was a man with his hands tied behind his back and his legs drawn up and tied to his body with thick ropes. Some of the men looked Dutch, others looked like Europeans. They were in green, many in torn up uniforms. The faces and bodies I saw were covered with blood. Another truck and several motorcycles with Japanese soldiers followed on. My mother and I heard later from Indonesians that the trucks first went to Ampelgading and from there along various estates roads back to the main road (the South Smeroe Road) and proceeded to Pasirian on the South Coast. I was told that the prisoners, alive and

> in baskets were thrown over the high cliffs into the sea at Pasirian at the spot where the ancient Indonesians had their place of sacrifices.

A Chinese man who was a merchant in Surabaya at the time was also a witness. He remembers:

> At two o'clock in the afternoon I was standing in the street Kapasan in front of the market, when I saw three trucks coming from the east. One truck stopped a few metres away from me. On the vehicle were a Japanese driver, two Japanese guards and many prisoners in pig baskets. Most of these men wore shorts or short underpants only. They were alive but in extremely weak condition and obviously very thirsty. I, with many others came as near as one metre from the truck, while the guards took their refreshments. All the prisoners were alive. One of the guards threw a bucket of water over and against the baskets but did not give them anything to drink.
>
> I saw a bundle of uniforms lying on the truck and some of the khaki shirts had two and three white stripes on the sleeves. This made me guess that some of the prisoners were perhaps British. The truck then drove away to the east.
>
> That same evening, I heard from my Indonesian friend Mr. K. who worked at the oil refinery in Wonokromo that a truck stopped on the other side of the canal (about thirty meters distance away from him). Japanese men took baskets with men in them out of the truck and threw them in the canal.

Ballalae Massacre, November 1942

In October 1942, six months after the fall of Singapore, 600 British prisoners of war, mostly Royal Artillery, under their commander Lieutenant Colonel John Bassett, were loaded onto the *Nagara Maru* in Keppel Harbour. They were told that they were to be shipped to Japan, but instead the ship headed south, stopping in Surabaya, Indonesia, and continuing to Rabaul on the island of New Britain, in Papua New Guinea. One man died on the voyage.

A month later, 517 of the fittest men in the party were shipped out of Rabaul, again on the *Nagara Maru*, and taken to Ballalae, an island of the Shortland Island Group in the Western Province of the Solomon Islands, where they were set to work building an airfield. Shortly after arriving, one of the prisoners, on disobeying an order, was beheaded by a Lieutenant Commander Ozaki Noriko.

On the night of 12/13 March 1943, during a raid by American B-24s, around 300 prisoners were killed when bombs landed on their camp. Three months later, another heavy air raid, followed by shelling from US Navy ships, convinced the Japanese that the island was about to be invaded. On 30 June, the remaining survivors, around 70 to 100 men, were all bayoneted or beheaded, with their bodies cremated.

After the war, the Japanese denied any knowledge of the executions, insisting that the 517 men shipped out of Rabaul had died when their ship was sunk and that the remaining men died in the bombing. This theory was debunked after the war when some Chinese and Korean prisoners working on the island reported the massacre. No war crime convictions for the massacre on Ballalae were ever made.

The Double Tenth Massacre, Singapore, October 1943

In September 1943, a group of Allied special forces led by Lieutenant Colonel Ivan Lyon, left Australia in a submarine on a mission called Operation Jaywick. Their objective was to attack the Japanese shipping moored in Singapore's Keppel Harbour.

Transferring from the submarine to junks in the Java Sea, they then used canoes to infiltrate the harbour, where, on 26 September, they sank seven Japanese ships with limpet mines before getting away safely back to Australia.

Meanwhile in Singapore, the Kempeitai, under the command of Lieutenant Colonel Haruzo Sumida, were convinced that the raid had been assisted by information sent to Australia from civilians and inmates of Changi prison using hidden radios. They descended on the prison and arrested fifty-seven prisoners, charging them with supplying information to the Allies, cutting of telephone lines and burning warehouses. Included in those arrested was an Anglican bishop, the Right Reverend Leonard Wilson, Bishop of Singapore, a former British colonial secretary and information officer, Rob Heely Scott, and a doctor called Cuthbert Stanley. After being interrogated by Warrant Officer Monai Tadamori, Scott was tortured into confessing that there was an anti-Japanese group in Singapore but said he knew nothing about Operation Jaywick. He was sentenced to six years in Outram Road Gaol.

During their search of the prison, the Kempeitai discovered a radio, resulting in the fifty-seven men being tortured. Subjected to beatings and torture, they had their hands tied behind their backs and were forced to kneel on sharp pieces of wood, and some had a metal bar placed behind their knees. The Japanese would then jump on them, forcing the wood and metal into their legs. Twelve died of sickness due to the appalling conditions during a seven-month period of incarceration. Three of the group taken from Changi prison were women, who were forced to share cells with male prisoners of all races and afforded no privacy even for their intimate requirements.

Doctor Stanley was executed as he was classed as a 'master spy'. Stanley's son, Nigel, who was 4 years old, managed to get away from Singapore with his mother before it fell, and it was not until a year later that his mother found out by reading about it in a newspaper article that her husband had been killed. She was devastated. I have met Nigel on numerous occasions.

One Singapore resident, Elizabeth Choy Su-Mei, along with her husband, decided to try to help the British internees who were suffering in Outram Road Gaol. The couple managed to get food, medicine, money, messages and even radios to the internees. When the Kempeitai searched the prison, they found parts for a radio that they were able to trace back to Choy. On 15 November 1943, along with her husband, she was arrested and held with twenty other women in the old YMCA building on Stamford Road. She was tortured constantly. Her husband was brought in to watch while she was kicked, beaten, and given electric shock treatment, but despite her suffering, she refused to confess that she had been helping the British prisoners. Six months later, the couple were finally released.

After the war, Elizabeth Choy talked about her experiences at the hands of the Kempeitai in Singapore:

> They stripped me to the waist and tied my hands and feet in such a way I couldn't move. That day they brought my husband to kneel beside the frame to watch me being tortured and they applied electricity on my bare back you know, oh I screamed and I had tears coming down, my nose running, it was terrible ... the Japanese asked us to give names of those who are anti-Japanese and then we would be set free at once, my husband said 'we don't know anybody', and so I said 'I don't know anybody'. All right you won't tell us, tomorrow we will take your husband to Johore Bahru to be executed at 9:00 o'clock and at 10:00 o'clock we

> will take you to Johore Bahru to be executed. So, they told us to say goodbye, so my husband said goodbye Elizabeth, don't worry, if we die, we die an honourable death.

Elizabeth Choi Su-Mei was awarded an Order of the British Empire for her heroic deeds in Singapore during the Japanese occupation, going on to become Singapore's first female legislator, a fashion model, and a schoolteacher.

At a war crimes tribunal on 18 March 1946, Elizabeth Choi was asked if Sumida should be executed for his deeds. She replied: no. The trial went on for four weeks, after which Sumida was sentenced to death despite her comments. Elizabeth Choy died in 2006 at the age of the 96.

Twenty-one members of the Kempeitai were tried from 18 March to 15 April 1946. The court found 14 of them guilty, with 8 sentenced to death by hanging, 6 to a serve a prison term, whilst 7 were acquitted.

Atrocities on Nauru, 1943–1945

In August 1942, the Japanese invaded the Australian-controlled Micronesian island of Nauru in the North Pacific. The island was not particularly strategic for the Japanese from a military perspective, but it had mining reserves of phosphate run by the British Phosphate Commission.

Most of the Australians on the island had left in February, except for five officials and two European missionaries. The native population was made up of about 1,800 Nauruans, 190 Gilbertese, 200 Chinese and a leper colony of 39 people. The Japanese took over the British Phosphate Commission, setting up their own company to mine the phosphate. To defend the island, they brought in 1,054 construction workers and embarked on building an airfield.

Seven months later, in March 1943, the US Air Force bombed the newly constructed airfield, destroying eight bombers and seven fighter planes of the Japanese Navy. In retaliation, the Japanese executed the five Australian officials.

The Japanese officer in charge, Lieutenant Nakayama, ordered Sub Lieutenant Sasaki Saburō, along with five other soldiers, to dig five graves on the beach. The five men were then driven in a truck to the site, where Nakayama himself beheaded one of them, before ordering the soldiers to behead the other four men. There is some doubt of course as to whether all five men were executed on the beach, as it has been alleged by other witnesses that one man was beheaded in a house.

Evidence for this was given after the war by a Gilbertese man called Tauna, who testified:

> At Daybreak, a motor truck came alongside the hospital, and I saw four Japanese soldiers, one carrying a sword and three with rifles, enter a house close to the hospital. One Japanese soldier opened the door of the house and called for them to come to the door and line up before him inside the house. Three Japanese with rifles stood outside the doorway of the house and the one with the sword was standing in front of them. The Japanese with the sword called one of them to step close to him. One man stepped forward and I saw him stoop over, and the Japanese raised his sword with one hand and brought it down on his neck. His head was severed from the rest of his body. Then Doctor Quinn, Mr Doyle, Mr Harmer, and Mr Shugg stepped forward one at a time, and the Japanese with the sword went through the same motion until all the men mentioned had been decapitated. After the execution, I saw each body being carried to a motor truck and placed in a large box therein.

Some other local people gave evidence that they saw Japanese soldiers hauling dead bodies out of the house, putting them into a truck, and driving away. Others, who visited the house later, saw bloodstains on the floors and walls. These people were threatened with beheading by the Japanese if they ever told anyone about it.

Living on an isolated part of the island were thirty-five lepers, looked after by a doctor called Bernicke. Leprosy became a problem on Nauru in the late 1920s, when around 30 per cent of the population had shown signs of the disease. By 1940, however, only around 8 per cent of the population were suffering from it. The Japanese were terrified about the spread of the disease and decided that all lepers in the occupied areas should be sent to an island called Pohnpei. The thirty-nine, including twenty-four men and fifteen women, were put on a small boat and towed by a ship called the *Shinsu Maru* out of Nauru on 11 July 1943. When the *Shinsu* was well out to sea, the tow rope was cut, and the small craft was then destroyed by cannon fire. Any survivors left in the water were shot by rifle fire.

The officer responsible for the beheadings and the deaths of the lepers, Lieutenant Nakayama, confessed after the war, on 5 May 1946, while detained in Rabaul. He was sentenced to death by an Australian Military Court and was hanged on 10 August that year. Sasaki was also tried for his involvement and was sentenced to twenty years' imprisonment.

Massacre on Palawan, December 1944

On 12 August 1942, 300 American prisoners of war, who had been taken prisoner after the battles of Bataan and Corregidor, were transported by ship to Palawan, an island 400 miles south-west of Manila in the Sulu Sea. For the next two years, they slaved under a cruel regime, building and maintaining an airfield for the Japanese.

In December 1944, when the island came under attack from American aircraft, the prisoners were herded into shelters in an enclosure on the cliffs overlooking the Bay of Puerto Princesa, where they were forced to dig trenches to be used as air raid shelters.

With the Americans now closing in on the island, the officer in command of Japanese troops, Captain Kojima, sought advice from senior officers as to what action to take regarding the prisoners. He was sent the following reply: 'At the time of the enemy landing, if the prisoners are harbouring an enemy feeling, dispose of them at the appropriate time.'

Wasting no time, Kojima ordered that the prisoners be herded into the trenches they had dug, gasoline poured over them and set alight. The skeletons were then buried on the beach. Only five of the men managed to escape, by jumping over cliffs and swimming across the bay to reach the safety of a Filipino guerrilla camp.

One of those five survivors, Gunnery Sergeant Douglas William Bogue of the United States Marine Corps, told his story after the war:

> As I was near the entrance of my shelter, I stuck my head out to see what was taking place. The first thing I saw was a black pillar of smoke coming from the entrance of A Company shelter. It appeared to me that about fifty to sixty Jap soldiers, armed with rifles, hand grenades, light machine-guns, and carrying torches and buckets containing gasoline, were attacking the A Company shelter which was next to mine. The buckets of gasoline were thrown into the entrance of the

> shelter and a lighted torch was then thrown in to ignite the gasoline: and, as the men were forced to come out on fire, they were bayoneted, shot, clubbed, or stabbed. I saw several men staggering about, still in flames, and saw them fall down shot. Some of the Japanese attacking force then branched off and attacked the north-east entrance of C Company's shelter and the north entrance of B Company's shelter. Due to the confined space, the whole attack was visible at a glance. I saw several Japanese shooting, and stabbing with their bayonets directly above where Stidham was lying helpless on a stretcher. I saw one man, whom I presumed to be Dr Mango, with his clothes smouldering, staggering towards the Japs with his arms outstretched, when he was mowed down by a Japanese soldier with a light machine-gun. Other American prisoners of war, who were coming out of these narrow entrances, were shot as they emerged, or mowed down as they made for the fence above the cliff.

Another of the survivors, Eugene Nielsen, also told his story after he managed to escape:

> The trench smelled very strongly of gas. There was an explosion and flames shot throughout the place. Some of the guys were moaning. I realized this was it – either I had to break for it or die. Luckily, I was in the trench closest to the fence. So I jumped and dove through the barbed wire. I fell over the cliff and somehow grabbed hold of a small tree … There were Japanese soldiers down on the beach. I buried myself in a pile of garbage and coconut husks. I kept working my way under until I got fairly covered up … The Japanese were bayoneting [prisoners on the beach]. They shot or stabbed twelve Americans and then dug a shallow grave in the sand and threw them in.

When he thought that the Japanese soldiers had disappeared, Nielsen jumped up from his covering, but as they were still there, he started running and was hit by rifle fire several times. Fortunately, he managed to survive by jumping into the sea and escaping. Despite his wounds, he swam for nine hours before eventually joining up with American forces.

After the war, the Japanese guard commander, Lieutenant Junsabura Toshino, was brought to trial, found guilty and sentenced to death by hanging.

The Kalagon Massacre, July 1945

As the war drew to a close in mid-1945, and with defeat almost inevitable, the Japanese embarked on a frenzy of even more atrocities. On 7 July, members of the 3rd Battalion 215th Regiment, along with the Moulmein Kempeitai, carried out atrocities against the inhabitants of Kalagon, a village near Tenasserim in Burma (present-day Myanmar).

During the previous few weeks, local guerrillas had been assisting British paratroopers landing in Burma. The Japanese were furious and proceeded to comb the area looking for anyone who might have helped them. The 3rd Battalion 215, after surrounding the village, rounded up the inhabitants and confined them in the local mosque for questioning. After being tortured to extract confessions that they had aided the British paratroopers, the Japanese commander, Major Ichikawa Seigi, ordered those found guilty to be killed.

The following morning, they were taken out and bayoneted or shot, with their bodies dumped into wells. Between 600 and 1,000 civilians were massacred on that fateful day. Those who managed to survive the massacre by escaping into the surrounding fields became witnesses in war crimes proceedings against the Japanese when the war ended.

One of the Japanese soldiers who carried out this atrocity on the people of Kalagon, Kubota Hisao, many years later told a newspaper that he had been haunted all his life with the memory of killing a boy of 14 or 15 on the orders of one of his officers. He said:

> I pulled the trigger immediately, like a machine … we were taught that the superior's order was the same as the emperor's. I didn't even hesitate, but I felt as if I was killing my little brother. All people who went to the war took part, directly or indirectly, in a massacre.

Operation Rimau Murders, Singapore, July 1945

After the success of Operation Jaywick, a special forces attack on Japanese shipping in Singapore's harbour in September 1943 (see page 144), the Allies launched a similar attack in October 1943 called Operation Rimau. The success of Jaywick encouraged them to embark on a further raid on Japanese shipping in Singapore's harbour. This attack was once again led by Ivan Lyon, by now a lieutenant colonel.

Lyon enlisted twenty-two experienced men to take part in a raid that was expected to be much more difficult than Jaywick, as the Japanese had increased their surveillance and defences in and around Keppel Harbour.

The group left the Australian port of Freemantle on 11 September 1944, in the submarine HMS *Porpoise*, arriving at Pulau Merapas, a tiny uninhabited island in the South China Sea, twelve days later, on the 23rd. The plan was to establish a base on the island with enough provisions to sustain them for three months. The raid on Singapore was scheduled for 10 October.

At Pulau Merapas, the aim was to capture a native boat, such as a junk, to sail them on to Singapore. On 28 September, the submarine spotted a junk called the *Mustika* and seven of the Rimau group boarded it and set sail for Singapore, approximately 90 miles away. When they neared Singapore, they transferred into ten folboats (folding canoes) and scuttled the junk.

On the night of 10/11 October, they reached Keppel Harbour and managed to blow up at least three ships before making their escape. The escape plan was to meet up with the submarine HMS *Tantalus* near one of the islands, but as their communications had broken down, they were forced to split up into groups and go on the run around the islands of the Riau Archipelago.

Ivan Lyon and two of the men were killed in a firefight on Soreh Island, whilst ten others also died trying to defend themselves. The remaining eleven men were eventually captured on another island, taken to Singapore in January 1945, and interned in Tanjong Pagar police station. There they were subjected to varying degrees of physical and mental abuse before being transferred to Outram Road Gaol in March, where one of them died from malaria. The others were beaten and tortured on a regular basis with swords, fists and feet. They existed on a starvation diet of around 500 grams of rice a day. One of them had his feet burned by a Japanese guard.

On 3 July, with the end of the war just about six weeks away, the remaining ten men were taken from Outram Road prison to Raffles College, the Japanese military headquarters in Singapore. There they stood trial on charges of 'perfidy and espionage'. It was highly unlikely that these men would be given a fair trial as it was alleged that they took part in military operations dressed as civilians, and indeed, they were found guilty and sentenced to death by beheading.

On Saturday, 7 July, they were taken from their cells at Outram Road Gaol and driven to some open ground on Bukit Timah Road in a bus with blacked-out windows. According to Japanese accounts:

> All of them were given cigarettes and rested. Then in accordance with their request, they were allowed to shake hands with each other. They all stood up, shook hands merrily and even laughingly in very harmonious air and bid farewell to each other; the sky was clear, and it was a very historic scenery.

The beheading of prisoners was seen by the Japanese as a great sporting event, and troops were lined up to watch the proceedings. When the men were brought forward to be beheaded, they were taunted by the soldiers looking on before being blindfolded and forced to kneel over three open graves. Their bodies were then thrown into the graves, one on top of another, four in one and three in each of the other two. They had been stripped of all badges of rank and identity discs, with nothing left to indicate who was buried there. Several days later, six wooden crosses were placed on top of the mounds of earth.

War crimes investigators adjudged that no war crime had been committed as:

> By being dressed in non-military attire, these intrepid Australians voluntarily deprived themselves of the right to be treated as prisoners according to the custom and usage of war. Technically, therefore, the Japanese did not commit a war crime and, accordingly, there is no means of bringing them to justice in this particular case.

Ironically, the Rimau heroes were avenged after the war. Although none of the Japanese responsible for their executions was charged with the atrocity, they faced charges for other war crimes. Four of the main offenders were hung: General Itagaki, commander-in-chief of the 7th Area Army, who had insisted on the death penalty; Major General Otsuka, who had been responsible for the legal proceedings; and the two commandants of Outram Road Gaol, Majors Mikizawa and Kobayashi.

(The commander of the military section of Outram Road Gaol, Major Shozo Kobayashi, faced charges over the deaths of around 1,500 prisoners in the prison, and at the war crimes tribunal, he was sentenced to death by hanging.)

The Loa Kulu Massacre, July 1945

Prior to the outbreak of the Second World War, the island of Borneo was divided between the British and the Dutch empires. When the Japanese invaded in March 1942, around 150 soldiers of the Royal Netherlands East Indies Army were taken prisoner, but for some reason, they were given restricted freedom in the city of Samarinda in the province of East Kalimantan, on the banks of the Mahakam River. They lived with their families for the next three years on the understanding that they would not take up arms again.

Their peaceful existence was rudely interrupted in July 1945, when they were all sentenced to death by a Japanese officer, with no reasons given. They were taken to Loa Kulu on the outskirts of Samarinda, where the men, along with their children, were forced to watch as their wives were cut to pieces with swords and bayonets. They were then forced to watch as the Japanese threw the screaming children down a 600-foot mineshaft, before the men themselves were lined up and beheaded. Their bodies were then all thrown down the mineshaft – another horrific atrocity carried out by the Japanese during the war.

Chapter 14

The Kempeitai

The Kempeitai (the Japanese counterpart of the Nazi Gestapo) was the most feared of all their forces during the Second World War. Founded in 1881, it was originally set up to ensure military discipline in the Japanese Army, but its role was extended during the early part of the twentieth century to cover the civilian population of Japan and then in the countries they annexed. Given supreme powers to arrest fifth columnists, make up propaganda programmes and squash any anti-Japanese feeling, the Kempeitai were feared by the Japanese people as well as the people in the annexed countries.

When the Japanese invaded the Philippines in December 1941, the Filipino population were terrified of the Kempeitai; to be arrested by them for whatever reason meant almost certain death. In Manila, Kempeitai prisons were set up, the most dreaded being Fort Santiago, known as the Bastille of Pasig, where Filipinos were subjected to physical and mental torture for being anti-Japanese.

In Allied prisoner of war camps all over South East Asia, the Kempeitai were hated and feared. Any prisoner found with a hidden radio, newspapers or personal diary was subjected to intense brutality and, in many cases, death. Food was a priority, just to keep themselves alive, for men like my father in the camps, but if they were caught stealing food, they were severely and brutally punished. In Havelock Road camp in Singapore, one British soldier, A.G. Allbury, recalled an incident when four of his friends were caught stealing rice while on dock duty:

> They dragged them out of the ranks and gave them the most savagely brutal beating up. Sweating and grunting, their vicious yellow faces distorted with rage, they continued to thud heavy boots into the prostrate figures on the ground long after the men had lost consciousness. The dockside, still smiling in the warm evening sun, became suddenly a terrible place to be in.

On the Japanese home islands, the Kempeitai were feared as much by the people themselves as by the prisoners. One British prisoner, James Allan Ford of the Royal Scots, remembered his time in a prison camp in Yokohama:

> I noticed that the Kempeitai were feared as much by the Japanese as by the prisoners. Although of comparatively junior rank they walked into camps or workplaces without hindrance and shouted orders at officers and civilians alike. They were swaggering bullies and used physical attack as a matter of course.

Another man who was imprisoned in camp 17 near Omuta, Kyushu, Roy Whitecross of the Australian 18th Division AIF, recalled when a prisoner called Hubbard was caught with a piece of Japanese newspaper:

> If he had been found carrying a bomb the Japanese could not have made more fuss. He was bashed by the entire guard and thrown into the aeso (guard house). The next day three Kempeitai corporals came to the camp. They beat Hubbard with their rifle butts. For four days Hubbard's screams echoed across the subdued camp – until merciful death claimed him at last.

On the island of Timor, occupied by the Japanese from February 1942, the Timorese paid a heavy price for their continued resistance to the invaders, with tens of thousands of civilians brutally murdered. In September 1944, after several members of the Kempeitai were killed, a Japanese officer called Shizuichi Tanaka ordered the Rajah of Loeang to produce the people responsible. When the Rajah refused to do this, he was executed, along with ninety-six other islanders taken at random.

When Dutch Sumatra fell to the Japanese in March 1942, the Kempeitai carried out brutal atrocities on the civilians. Women and children were taken away from their husbands and put into separate camps. In one camp at Brastagi, the women were so incensed by the lack of food that when several hundred of them tried to break out to obtain supplies, they were quickly rounded up and subjected to beatings. One of the women, a nurse called Verpleegster Schuddeboum, was beaten with a wooden curtain rail. Another woman, Mevrouw Prins, told what happened next:

> I was thrown into a cell with another woman that did not have light or ventilation. The floor was running with urine and there was excreta on the walls. The following morning, I was taken to a room where two members of the Kempeitai were standing. After being interrogated, I was made to stand on a chair with my hands tight behind my back with a rope over my head until I could hardly reach the seat of the chair with the points of my toes. He kept on raising and lowering me until my arms were nearly pulled out of their sockets. He asked me to plead guilty and each time I give the wrong answer he beat me on my back with a rubber truncheon. I was then taken back to my cell where the Japanese warder push me in with so much force that I fell flat on my face on the filthy floor and lay there for a long time completely stunned.

The next day, Mrs Prins was told that she was to be executed. She and two other women were taken to a room where they were made to stand facing a wall with their arms behind their backs. When she heard rifle bolts being opened and closed, Mrs Prins prayed and waited for the bullets, but nothing happened and they were released.

The cruelty of the Kempeitai knew no boundaries, as such treatment handed out because a group of women went out of the camp to look for food for their children illustrates.

Elizabeth van Kampen, a young Dutch girl of 14, was living with her family on a rubber plantation in Java when the Japanese invaded the island in March 1942 (see The Pig Basket Atrocity, page 141). For the next eleven months, the van Kampens were left to live their lives pretty much as normal; her father was a useful asset to the Japanese, being the manager of a rubber plantation. At the beginning of February 1943, along with many other Dutch national men, her father, Theo van Kampen, was taken away from his family to an all-male internment camp, leaving Elizabeth's mother alone to look after three young girls. Their blissfully happy childhoods soon turned into a nightmare. For almost three years, the van Kampens experienced hunger, terror, violence, deaths of friends and eventually that of their own beloved father at the hands of the Kempeitai. The Japanese were no respecters of race or sex, and treated the Dutch men and women with contempt and cruelty. Elizabeth van Kampen harboured a hatred of the Kempeitai for the rest of her life as she is convinced that they murdered her father. She makes this quite clear in her book *Two Years of Tenko Life as a 16-year-old in a Japanese Prisoner of War Camp.*

In February 1945, as the Allies were trying to push the Japanese back through Burma towards Thailand, a British RAF Liberator crashed in the Pengu district of southern Burma. The crew of six were captured and taken to the Kempeitai headquarters, where they were interrogated and tortured before being taken out to a trench, blindfolded, and decapitated by an officer.

In May 1945, a US airman was shot down near Saigon in French Indochina and captured by the Kempeitai. After three days of intense questioning and torture, they ordered doctors to dispose of him by injecting him with a large dose of novocaine.

Most former members of the Kempeitai were reluctant to talk about what they did during the war, but one man called Yoshio Tshuchiya did open up later, when he said:

> Most interrogations would begin by beating the suspect with fists or a stick, but beatings exhaust us, so we move on to torture. Then the victim might be attacked with a red-hot iron bar. The iron bar was brought in, and it was all red with heat and it was hard to stay in the room because human flesh burns and it smells bad. Sometimes we used hanging torture in which a large stone was tied to the suspect's body and he was suspended in a position of excruciating agony for hours at a time. This was not as effective as water torture. You tie them face up lying on a long bench then you put a cloth on the face and then you pour water onto the cloth so the person can't help drinking it. You push their stomach out with water, blow it right up. When the stomach is distended, we would beat the victim hard on the belly with a stick, so the water was vomited up. During the torture some people are killed. We try not to kill them but to take them to the verge of being killed.

When the Second World War was drawing to a close in mid-1945, the Kempeitai began to increase their cruelty towards prisoners and local populations. Even after the war ended, on 15 August 1945, they carried on killing prisoners of war. At Ranau in Borneo, thirty remaining prisoners of war were murdered even though the Japanese understood the war was over.

The following is an extract from a captured Kempeitai booklet entitled *How to Interrogate.* Among the instructions was:

> Measures to be normally adopted. – Torture (COMMON) (embraces beating, kicking, and all conduct involving physical suffering). It is the clumsiest method and only to be used, when all else fails. Then violent torture is used change interrogation officers and it is beneficial if one new officer questions in a sympathetic fashion. Threats. As a hint of physical discomforts to come, e.g. murder, torture; starving, deprivation of sleep, solitary confinement, etc. Mental discomforts to come, e.g. will not receive same treatment as other prisoners of war; in event of exchange of prisoners he will be kept till last; he will be forbidden to send letters; will be forbidden to inform his home he is prisoner of war.

When Japan surrendered in August 1945, records were deliberately destroyed, making it difficult to identify prominent Kempeitai officers, many of them going underground to avoid prosecution at the war crimes tribunals.

Chapter 15

War Crimes Tribunals, 1946–1951

When the Second World War started, at the beginning of December 1941 the Allies made it quite clear to the Japanese that they would be held answerable for any atrocities carried out during the conflict. The Japanese government were certainly left in no doubt as to what the consequences would be if they lost the war.

On 26 July 1945, United States President Harry S. Truman, United Kingdom Prime Minister Winston Churchill, and Chiang Kai-shek of China signed the Potsdam Declaration. It called for the surrender of all Japanese armed forces and outlined the terms of surrender for the Empire of Japan. It stated that, if Japan did not surrender, it would face 'prompt and utter destruction'. Its terms read:

1. There must be eliminated for all time the authority and influence of those who have deceived and misled the people of Japan into embarking on world conquest.
2. We do not intend that Japan be enslaved as a race or destroyed as a nation, but stern justice shall be meted out to all war criminals including those who have visited cruelties upon our prisoners.

When Japan surrendered on 15 August 1945, their government and military moved swiftly to destroy any evidence that might assist in the prosecution of those responsible for war crimes. By the time that the surrender was formally signed in Tokyo Bay on 2 September 1945, most Japanese records relating to war crimes had been destroyed.

On 8 October 1945, a mere two months after the war ended, the first of the war crimes trials against the Japanese commenced in Manila. The most notorious Japanese officer put on trial was General Yamashita Tomoyuki, who was in command of troops at the 'Rape of Manila'. (See Chapter 3.) Although he was not in the city at the time, and communications with his frontline officers had been cut, Yamashita was found guilty of failing to prevent the massacres and atrocities in the Philippines and was sentenced to death.

Yamashita's case, in respect of a commander's responsibilities, set a precedent throughout the many war crimes tribunals that were to follow, and it became known as the Yamashita standard.

On 29 April 1946, eleven countries came together to form the International Military Tribunal for the Far East (IMTFE), a tribunal that was convened to try the Japanese leaders for joint conspiracy to start and wage war, and for the atrocities that they had committed. The IMTFE was modelled on the International Military Tribunal (IMT), formed several months earlier in Nuremberg, Germany, to prosecute senior officials of Nazi Germany.

The eleven countries involved were: Australia, Canada, China, France, India, the Netherlands, New Zealand, the Philippines, the Soviet Union, the United Kingdom, and the United States.

The British went on to set up 330 war crimes tribunals to deal with war crimes committed in different locations across Asia, including Singapore, Indonesia, Cambodia, Thailand, Myanmar, and the Andaman and Nicobar Islands. Of these, 131 were conducted in Singapore, with others set up in Kuala Lumpur, Rangoon, Hong Kong and Borneo. They also set up 'travelling courts' that made their way to various locations to hear a case. The tribunals set up three categories of war crimes:

Class A charges:	alleged crimes against peace, to be brought against Japan's top leaders who had planned and directed the war.
Class B and C charges:	to be levelled at Japanese of any rank, covering conventional war crimes and crimes against humanity, respectively.

The defendants brought to trial were accused of promoting a scheme that:

> Contemplated and carried out … murdering, maiming and ill-treating prisoners of war (and) civilian internees … forcing them to labour under inhumane conditions … plundering public and private property, wantonly destroying cities, towns and villages beyond any justification of military necessity; (perpetrating) mass murder, rape, pillage, brigandage, torture and other barbaric cruelties upon the helpless civilian population of the over-run countries.

Historian Richard B. Finn writes about the war crimes tribunals in his book *Winners in Peace*:

> World War II was the first major conflict in history in which the victors carried out trials and punishment of thousands of persons in the defeated nations for 'crimes against peace' and 'crimes against humanity', two new and broadly defined categories of international crime.

Whilst war crime tribunals were held in various countries across the Far East, the main trials took place in Tokyo, under the leadership of General MacArthur. They began on 3 May 1946 and lasted two and a half years. Other tribunals were held in cities throughout Asia and the Pacific between 1945 and 1948. Around 5,600 Japanese personnel were prosecuted during more than 2,200 trials, about 1,000 of them being found guilty and sentenced to death. The largest single trial was that of ninety-three Japanese military personnel charged with the execution of over 300 Allied prisoners of war in the Ambon Island massacre. (See page 134).

A trial got underway in Labuan in late 1945, when the Japanese responsible for the Sandakan death marches (see Chapter 12) were charged with crimes committed against prisoners of war during the forced marches. A Japanese sergeant called Hosotani Naoji, found guilty of shooting two Australian prisoners and five ethnic Chinese civilians, was sentenced to death, and executed by firing squad on 6 March 1946.

It was not just Japanese military who were put on trial after the war. Many high-ranking civilians were also tried, including three former prime ministers: Kōki Hirota, Hideki Tōjō and Kuniaki Koiso. All three men were convicted of Class A war crimes. Koreans were also tried for war crimes, with 148 convicted and imprisoned, the most prominent being Lieutenant General Hong Sa-ik. Hong Sa-ik was found guilty of war crimes against American and Filipino prisoners and was sentenced to death. He was hanged in Manila in September 1945.

One hundred and sixty Taiwanese who had served in the forces of the Empire of Japan were also convicted, eleven being executed.

The Chinese also launched war crimes tribunals against the Japanese, in particular for those involved in the Rape of Nanking, whilst France and the Netherlands put Japanese soldiers on trial for atrocities on Java and for forcing many women into comfort stations.

The main international military tribunal in Tokyo delivered its judgement on Japanese aggression when it concluded in 1948:

> During the period of several months the tribunal had heard evidence from a large number of witnesses who testified in detail to atrocities committed in all theatres of war on a scale so vast, yet following so common a pattern, only one conclusion is possible. The atrocities were either secretly ordered or wilfully permitted by the Japanese government or individual members thereof, and by leaders of the armed forces.

Whilst many Japanese war criminals who were charged went unpunished, thousands were prosecuted. Prime Minister General Tōjō Hideki was hanged. Sixteen others were sentenced to life imprisonment (of whom four died in prison) and two received lesser terms. After Tōjō Hideki was hanged in Sugamo Prison on 23 December 1948, his body was placed in a wooden coffin and taken to Yokohama Municipal Crematorium for cremation, his ashes scattered to the four winds. During his trial he desperately tried to deflect blame from himself and said:

> We did not even suspect that such things had happened. The emperor, especially, because of his benevolence, would have had a contrary feeling. Such acts are not permissible in Japan; the character of the Japanese people is such that they believe that neither heaven or earth would permit such things. It will be too bad if people in the world believes that these inhumane acts are the result of the Japanese character.

This statement seems to me to have been utter hypocrisy, as Tōjō has been described as: 'the most prominent and most blameworthy of all the major Japanese war criminals'.

When the Japanese surrendered Wake Island on 4 September 1945 (see page 124), Admiral Sakaibara and fifteen of his men were sent to Kwajalein to be tried for the murder of the American civilians. At his trial, Sakaibara confessed that he had ordered the execution of the ninety-eight Americans and was sentenced to death by a US Naval Court. He was hanged on Guam on 19 June 1947, with his last statement before he died filled with Japanese stoicism: 'I think my trial was entirely unfair and the proceedings unfair, and the sentence too harsh, but I obey with pleasure.'

When questioned in Manila during his trial for the Rape of Nanking, Lieutenant General Yamashita stated that he had never heard of the Singapore Alexandra Hospital Massacre (see Chapter 7) until that moment. As the hospital was in the line of advance of Lieutenant General Mutaguchi's 55th Regiment, Yamashita suggested that *he* should be questioned on this issue, not him. As stated earlier, Yamashita was found guilty and hanged anyway.

When Mutaguchi was interrogated at the trials by Colonel Wild, the interview went as follows:

Wild: On 12 February, troops of your 18th Division entered the hospital and started shooting and bayoneting everyone at sight. In the operating theatre they bayoneted a patient on the operating table and the surgeon who was operating on him. They killed both of these and wounded another medical officer and a medical orderly. After killing a lot more medical personnel and wounded, they collected over 200 as prisoners from the hospital and took them about half mile away, where they were locked up in some very small rooms. The next day they took them out and machine-gunned or bayoneted all but five, who escaped and become prisoners of war. The total number murdered in this hospital was over twenty medical officers, over sixty medical orderlies and over 200 wounded.

Mutaguchi: Are you sure it was the 18th Division?

Wild: Yes, I am.

Mutaguchi: Is that so? I never heard of it until today.

Wild: Well last October, I flew to Manila and told this story to General Yamashita. He told me that it must have been men of the 18th Division who did what he called 'this horrible and senseless thing'. He said that you must have heard of the massacre on such a scale as this and he himself advised me to ask for your explanation of it.

Mutaguchi: I never heard of it until now. I am astonished to hear it.

Wild: The senior officer, a Major General or Lieutenant General, went into the hospital the next day and told Colonel Craven that he was sorry about what had happened. In fact, he made some sort of apology and said, 'some of our men have no sense.' He also said that Colonel

Craven should regard his visit as an honour, as he was the representative of the Emperor of Japan. Was that you?

Mutaguchi: I never heard of it. I am surprised if Japanese soldiers did this.

Mutaguchi was convicted of war crimes and sentenced to imprisonment, later to be released from prison in March 1948 and returned to Japan.

Lieutenant General Homma was charged as a war criminal for his part in the murder of American and Filipino prisoners of war during the Bataan Death March (see Chapter 8). He was found guilty and was executed in 1946.

Vice Admiral Sakonju and Captain Mayuzumi were put on trial in Hong Kong charged with giving the order to execute the crew and passengers of the *Behar* (see page 81). Sakonju was sentenced to death and Mayuzumi to seven years' imprisonment.

Captain Hoshijima Susumu, the Sandakan prison commandant (see Chapter 12), his successor, Captain Takakuwa, and his second-in-command, Captain Watanabe Genzo, were all found guilty of war crimes and hanged at Rabaul on 6 April 1946.

In 1946, at a British military war crimes tribunal in Rangoon, Major Ichikawa Seigi and thirteen Japanese soldiers were tried for participating in the Kalagon massacre (see page 150). The charges against them were:

1. Participating in the massacre of the villagers.
2. Participating in the beating, torture, wounding, and other maltreatment of the villagers.

Seigi also faced a third charge for kidnapping women for sexual pleasure. Seven of them were found guilty on both counts, with three others found guilty on the second count. Seigi was found guilty on all counts and was hanged on 15 July 1946, whilst the three others were to be shot. Their sentence was later reduced to ten years' imprisonment in Rangoon Jail.

When Major General Saburō Kawamura was tried at the Singapore War Trials in 1947, he was found guilty and hanged for crimes committed during the Singapore Chinese massacre (see Chapter 5). Lieutenant General Takuma Nishimura was also found guilty of his part in the massacre, as well as for atrocities committed against Australian and Indian troops during fighting in Malaya in January 1941. He was also hanged.

Prince Nashimoto Morimasa, a member of the Japanese Imperial Family and a field marshal in the Imperial Japanese Army, was arrested for war crimes. His arrest caused great unrest among the Japanese people as it opened the door to the possibility that Emperor Hirohito and other senior members of the imperial household might also face prosecution for war crimes. Nashimoto was imprisoned in Tokyo's Sugamo Prison for four months, before the American authorities released him on 13 April 1946.

The Japanese officer in charge at the time of the Bangka Island massacre (see Chapter 9), Captain Orita, ended up in Russian hands after the war ended. He was handed over to the Australians in Tokyo and put on trial for the atrocity, but committed suicide in his cell before a judgement was made.

General Iwane Matsui, commander of the expeditionary force sent to China in 1937, was found guilty of war crimes and executed by the Allies for his involvement in the Nanjing Massacre. He was executed by hanging, his remains later interred at Yasukuni Shrine in 1978.

After the war, some survivors of the Singapore Chinese massacre (see Chapter 5) gave evidence to a war crimes tribunal in 1947. At the same tribunal, Japanese Army commanders testified that the man behind the massacre of the Chinese people in Singapore was Lieutenant Colonel Masanobu Tsuji, and that he had personally overseen many of the murders. Tsuji fled, first to Thailand and then to China, thus avoiding the trials, and was not prosecuted as a war criminal. A British Military Court sentenced his understudy, Lieutenant General Takuma Nishimura, to life imprisonment, but at a later trial, an Australian Military Court handed down the death sentence to him. Nishimura was hanged on 11 June 1951. Major General Kawamura Saburō was also sentenced to life imprisonment.

The commander-in-chief of Japanese forces in Java, Lieutenant General Hitoshi Imamura, was later acquitted of this atrocity in a Netherlands court for lack of evidence. A subsequent Australian Military Court found General Hitoshi Imamura responsible and handed down a sentence of ten years' imprisonment. He was imprisoned at Sugamo from 1946 to 1954.

Most of the Japanese who carried out atrocities were members of the armed forces, whilst the number of civilians tried for atrocities were mostly medical physicians working with the Japanese Army.

Whilst there seems no doubt, as I have clearly pointed out earlier in the book, that Emperor Hirohito was aware of atrocities carried out in the name of his country, he was never tried for war crimes. The Australian government wanted to put him on trial, but General Douglas MacArthur refused this on the basis that by keeping the emperor in place, the Japanese people were more likely to co-operate with the Americans. President Truman backed MacArthur, and Hirohito escaped prosecution solely on the grounds of political expediency. Many Japanese believed because of this that Hirohito was not a war criminal. From that inference, it was only a short step to a conclusion that, if the emperor was innocent, then Japan, as a nation, was also free from guilt. Most of the population believed that Japan's military aggression and war crimes could be laid at the door of the Imperial Japanese Army, which had betrayed the emperor and his people.

MacArthur's decision not to prosecute Hirohito for war crimes threw the whole legal credibility of the Tokyo War Crimes Tribunal into doubt. John Dower, in his book *Embracing Defeat*, said that 'the cover-up orchestrated by MacArthur turned the issue of war responsibility into a joke'.

Almost without exception, the war crimes tribunals adhered to the principle that any accused must be found innocent unless it can be proved 'beyond a reasonable doubt' that he is guilty of a specific, individual (as opposed to collective) offence.

The war crimes tribunals carried out at the end of the Second World War have long since faded into history, particularly from the Japanese position of denial and historical revision, but evidence has emerged that details the many tortures and atrocities carried out on a vast scale. It is only possible to draw one conclusion: that they were carried out with the knowledge and consent of the Japanese government.

When the trials concluded, neither Western nor Japanese governments seemed interested in taking Japan's war crimes further, in contrast to continued prosecution of Nazi war criminals in Western Europe. Further pressure was exerted by former prisoners of war such as my father, along with a small number of popular historians.

For many years after the war, when confronted by advocacy and human rights groups, the Japanese government insisted the issue of compensation for people affected by atrocities had been settled by the signing of the peace treaty in San Francisco in September 1951.

Not only did Japanese authorities refuse to acknowledge any wartime responsibility, but several conservative politicians and senior bureaucrats went so far as to publicly denounce the accusations as groundless historical revisionism and Japan-bashing.

Many people around the world were convinced that the US government engaged in a cover-up to conceal incriminating documents relating to war crimes in order not to embarrass the post-war Japanese government. Many searches were made to try to uncover classified materials, conducted independently of outside political interference of any sort. They found no evidence to support such assertions.

Chapter 16
Conclusion

'War is Hell,' said William Tecumseh Sherman, a general in the Union Army during the American Civil War (1861–1865).

'Dilemmas of war occur when decent people feel that they have no choice but to do terrible things. In total war, everybody becomes a combatant.'

Sherman was probably right, but the evillest part of hell has often been reserved for civilians, who in most cases took no part in wars. Women and children have been caught up in conflicts with the screaming, terror, brutality and trauma so very familiar over many centuries. The International Red Cross succinctly set out guidelines for behaviour in wars to try to protect innocent people:

> You do not attack civilians. You limit as much as you can the impact of your warfare on women and children, as well as on other civilians. You treat detainees humanely. You do not torture people. It protects Persons who do not, or no longer, take part in the fighting (including civilians, medics, aid workers, wounded, sick and shipwrecked troops, prisoners of war or other detainees), and imposes limits on the means and methods of warfare (for instance, the use of certain weapons) should be protected.

The Japanese, of course, as you will have read in every single page of this book, completely ignored this.

Hannah Arendt, a political philosopher, author and Holocaust survivor, coined the phrase 'the banality of evil'. She likened it to the personalities of men who performed acts of great evil and inhumanity. She was of course applying it to Nazis such as Adolph Eichmann, but indeed, she could well have been applying it to some of the Japanese military during the period I have examined.

John Glenn Gray, an American veteran of the Second World War, wrote about the satisfaction soldiers experience in sloughing off responsibility:

> Becoming a soldier was like escaping from one's own shadow. When I raised my right hand and took that oath, I freed myself of the consequences for what I do. I'll do what they tell me, and nobody can blame me.

In February 1944, when the war was starting to turn against them, Japanese Prime Minister Tōjō Hideki made an emergency declaration to the Japanese people to demand that '*gyokusai*' be carried out, a demand that instructed the entire Japanese population to be prepared to die if the Allies invaded their islands. Japan's mainland population at that time was 70 million, so in effect, he was ordering them all to die for the cause.

In June 1945, when Japan was on its knees, one senior Japanese officer was heard to say:

> Due to the nationwide food shortage and the imminent invasion of the home islands it will be necessary to kill all the infirmed old people, the very young and the sick, we cannot allow Japan to perish because of them.

Army chief of staff, General Korechika Anami, also said: 'Would it not be wondrous for the whole Japanese nation to be destroyed like a beautiful flower?'

Some of the dreadful atrocities I have outlined in this book are so disturbing that many people will shrink from picturing them. I have already detailed in my introduction the militarist approach in Japanese schools during the early part of the twentieth century, but one must ask, what caused the Japanese military to embark on such violence during the war years? Was it perhaps something more primal? Or indeed to do with the evolution of man? Historians and sociologists have come up with three possible answers to this question. Firstly, could wartime rape be a form of male bonding between soldiers? Secondly, could it be political – a means of breaking down the enemy's morale and that sense of identity? Or thirdly, is that it is part of masculinity itself?

This thought has been put forward by the American feminist writer Susan Brownmiller, who suggests: 'War provides men with the perfect psychological backdrop to give vent to their contempt for women. Men who rape are ordinary Joes, made more ordinary by entry into the most exclusive male only club in the world.'

It has also been suggested by historians that there were two main reasons:

1) The cruel treatment that the Japanese military meted out to their own soldiers.
2) The various layers of Japanese society with their unflinching worship of the emperor.

Ordinary Japanese soldiers were themselves subjected to humiliation. It has been said that Japanese soldiers had to wash the dirty underwear of their officers and stand to attention while they were bashed around the head for any small misdemeanour. The Japanese military treatment of both civilians and prisoners of war leaves us with a history that is intriguing and complex.

Historians have estimated that that between 1932 and 1945, the Japanese military regime murdered somewhere between 3 million and 10 million people. Some say that their actions may have been due to a combination of factors, including a morally bankrupt political and military strategy, military expediency, and custom and national culture.

After the war in Europe, Germany agreed a variety of treaties with countries to compensate the victims of the Holocaust with up to around €63 billion paid to individuals by 2005. Japan, however, has continued to deny its atrocities and has refused to pay compensation to any of its victims.

Right up until today, many Japanese people fail to understand why neighbouring countries still harbour grudges against them for events that happened during the 1930s and 1940s. The atrocities I have outlined in this book are still denied by many people in Japan. United States historian Allan Nevins noted: 'Probably in all our history no foe has been so detested as were the Japanese.'

Harold Timperley, in his book *Japan: a World Problem*, said:

> Megalomaniacal ideas have been working in the blood of the Japanese, not merely for generations, but for centuries. Feudal Bushido mentality, which prevented Japan from accepting Christian values in Western democracy, remains strong in Japan.

Since the end of the Second World War, in the Far East, government officials, scholars and former military officers of all ranks have denied and downplayed the atrocities committed by their military forces. In 1994, Japanese Minister of Justice Shigeto Nagano described the 1937 Nanking Massacre as a 'fabrication', and in 2007, Prime Minister Shinzo Abe denied that women had been forced into becoming military sex slaves. Some senior Japanese government officials, however, have issued numerous apologies for the country's war crimes. Japan's Ministry of Foreign Affairs stated:

> The country acknowledges its role in causing tremendous damage and suffering during World War II, especially in regard to the IJA entrance into Nanjing during which Japanese soldiers killed a large number of non-combatants and engaged in looting and rape.

Questioned after the war, Japanese veterans would usually try to explain acts of cruelty by saying, 'We were doing it for the emperor, he was our God.'

During the early months of 1945, when Japan realised that it was losing the war and an invasion of its home islands by the Americans was likely, their military hierarchy feared that large numbers of prisoners across the plethora of camps in the Far East might revolt and interfere with their final defence. Consequently, an order was sent out to every camp commander that all prisoners were to be annihilated, with all evidence destroyed. A copy of the order was found in United States archives after the war:

> The Time: Although the basic aim is to act under superior orders, individual disposition may be made in the following circumstances:
>
> 1. When an uprising of large numbers cannot be suppressed without the use of firearms.
> 2. When escapees from the camp may turn into a hostile fighting force.
>
> The Methods:
> 1. Whether they are destroyed individually or in groups, or however it is done, with mass bombing, poisonous smoke, poisons, drowning, decapitation, or what, dispose of them as the situation dictates.
> 2. In any case it is the aim not to allow the escape of a single one, to annihilate them all, and leave not any traces.

When I first came across this document, the hairs on the back of my neck stood on end, as this was, in effect, my father's death warrant. The dropping of the atomic bombs on Hiroshima and Nagasaki by the Americans saved his life. When anyone tries to tell me that the dropping of those bombs were also atrocities, I point them to my father's death warrant above. It is also worth pointing out that Japan was also working on the production of an atomic bomb under the aegis of a Dr Yoshio Nishina, a protégé of the great Danish particle physicist Niels Bohr. One of Nishina's colleagues said: 'If we'd built the bomb first, of course we would have used it.'

Had the bombs not been dropped, the Japanese were determined to defend their islands with 12,000 kamikaze pilots, 2.5 million troops and 28 million civilians armed with bamboo spears. It was only the intervention of Emperor Hirohito that forced the military leaders to surrender and thereby saved the lives of close to a million Allied troops and the 140,000 prisoners of war that Japan planned to murder if their country was invaded. The dropping of the atomic bombs also spared the lives of an estimated 5 to 10 million Japanese.

Controversial evidence has emerged in recent years that Japan surrendered not because of the dropping of the two atomic bombs, but because the Soviet Union entered the war. Its leaders were concerned that the country, if occupied by the Russians, would become a communist state. Japanese leaders said the bomb forced them to surrender because it was less embarrassing to say they had been defeated by a miracle weapon. Americans wanted to believe it, and the myth of nuclear weapons was born.

As the war drew to a close in August 1945, the Japanese attempted to erase any records of atrocities they carried out between 1931 and 1945, but a huge number of diaries and documents emerged later.

Whilst this book is subtitled *Japanese Military Atrocities*, it is widely assumed that their military leaders made the decisions to go to war, but evidence proves that this was not the whole story. As mentioned earlier, Emperor Hirohito himself had blood on his hands, as he was aware of what was happening across South East Asia and did little to prevent the atrocities being carried out in the name of Japan.

Most of the surviving Far East prisoners of war, such as my father, would never forgive or forget their treatment at the hands of the Japanese. In 1971, twenty-five years after the war ended, the Japanese sent Emperor Hirohito on a state visit to Britain, a visit that aroused intense feelings amongst the FEPOWS, and indeed in Lord Mountbatten, who after initially refusing to attend, was persuaded by the queen to take part. Thousands of protesters lined the route to Buckingham Palace. Some turned their back on the emperor and wore red gloves to symbolise those who had died in the camps, while others whistled the popular Second World War march 'Colonel Bogey'.

Lieutenant General Shiro Ishii, the Japanese microbiologist in charge of Unit 731 (see Chapter 1), was an imperial prince and cousin of Emperor Hirohito, whilst his younger brother, Prince Mikasa, also viewed films taken in the unit. Mikasa wrote in his memoirs that he was also shown films of Chinese prisoners being marched out onto the Manchurian Plain as guinea pigs for gross experimentation on live subjects.

According to a Japanese journalist called Seiya Matsuno, Hirohito signed orders permitting the use of chemical weapons in China during 1938. Matsuno alleges that he also authorised the use of toxic gas on numerous occasions and that he had discovered an official report to prove it. This official report, compiled by a frontline nerve gas battalion of the Japanese Army posted in northern China, recorded that the unit used munitions containing a blister agent and a sternutatory agent.

During their years of captivity under a harsh regime, my father and his fellow prisoners of war went to the edge of a cliff and looked over; some, like he, managed to avoid being swept over, whilst many others not so fortunate were swept away. Those who suffered at the hands of the Japanese military and were lucky enough to survive the horrors were scarred for the rest of their lives. Many of the families of former prisoners of war have also been greatly affected by their relative's experiences, as Louise Cordingly points out in her excellent book *Echoes of Captivity*. Louise has interviewed many children of Far East prisoners of war including myself, and she sums it up beautifully when she says:

> For many (prisoners) the war did not end in 1945. For decades to come, the former prisoners had nightmares and flashbacks. Their wives and families struggled to cope with damaged men who couldn't find the words to talk about their experiences. These echoes of captivity carried on right to the end of the survivors' lives – and continue today in the lives of their children.

My father, and his colleagues who came back from the Far East when the war ended, were humbled by their experiences and I have every respect for not only their courage, but also for their humility.

A Prayer of Prisoners of War Who Survived the Japanese Camps

And we that are left grow old with the years
Remembering the heartache, the pain and the tears
Hoping and praying that never again
Men will sink to such sorrow and shame
The price that was paid we will always remember
Every day, every month and not just in November
We will remember them

Bibliography

All Hands magazine article, 'The March of Death', March 1944

Archer, Bernice & Fedorowich, Kent, 'The Women of Stanley: Internment in Hong Kong 1942–45', tandfonline.com/doi/abs/10.1080/09612029600200119

Azuma Shiro, *A Diary* (translated by Kimberly Hughes and published by the Phoenix Publishing Media Group)

Barber, Stephen, *Sadists of the Rising Sun*, Elektron Books, 2011

Barenblatt, Daniel, *A Plague Upon Humanity,* Souvenir Press, London, 2004

Bayley, Christopher & Harper, Tim, *Forgotten Armies: The Fall of British Asia, 1941–1945*, Penguin Books, London, 2005

Beattie, Rod, *The Death Railway: A brief History of the Thailand–Burma Railway*, TBRC Kanchanaburi, 2005

Behr, Edward, *Hirohito: Behind the Myth*, Penguin Books, London, 1989

Brooke, Geoffrey, *Singapore's Dunkirk*, Pen & Sword, Barnsley, 1989

Carew, Tim, *The Fall of Hong Kong*, Pan Books, London, 1963

Carey, John, *Eyewitness to History*, Avon Books, 1987

Chang, Iris, *The Rape of Nanking*, Basic Books, New York, 1997

Cordingly, Louise, *Echoes of Captivity*, High Winds Publishing, London, 2020

Craigie, Sir Robert, *Behind the Japanese Mask*, Hutchinson & Co., London, 1945

Dawes, James, *Evil Men*, Harvard University Press, Massachusetts, 2013

De Jong, Louis, *The Collapse of a Colonial Society: The Dutch in Indonesia during the Second World War*, KITLV Press, 2002

Drea, Edward, *Researching Japanese War Crimes Records*, Greg Bradsher, Robert Hanyok, James Lide, Michael Petersen, Daqing Yang, Nazi War Crimes and Japanese Imperial Government Records, Interagency Working Group, Washington, DC, published by the National Archives and Records Administration for the Nazi War Crimes and Japanese Imperial Government Records Interagency Working Group, 2006

Dyess, William, *The Dyess Story*, Verdun Press, 2014

Edwards, Bernard, *Blood and Bushido*, Brick Tower Press, New York, 1997

Felton, Mark, *Japan's Gestapo*, Pen & Sword Military, Barnsley, 2009

Felton, Mark, *The Final Betrayal, Mountbatten, MacArthur and the Tragedy of Japanese POWs*, Pen & Sword Military, Barnsley, 2010

Felton, Mark, *Slaughter at Sea*, Pen & Sword, Barnsley, 2007

Felton, Mark, *Children of the Camps*, Pen & Sword, Barnsley, 2011

Finn, Richard B., *Winners in Peace: MacArthur, Yoshida, and Postwar Japan*, University of California Press, 1992

Friedman, Sylvia Yu, *Silenced No More*, independently published, 2015

Harmsen, Peter, *Shanghai 1937: Stalingrad on the Yangtze*, Casemate, Oxford, 2013

Henling Wade, Tom, *Prisoner of the Japanese: From Changi to Tokyo*, Kangaroo Press, Nashville, 1994

Keith, Agnes, *Three Came Home*, Eland Publishing, London, 2002
Kennedy, Joseph, *Andy Dillon's Ill-Fated Division*, United Writers, Cornwall, 2000
Kovner, Sarah, *Prisoners of the Empire: Inside Japanese POW Camps*, Harvard University Press, 2020
Lamont-Brown, Raymond, *Kempeitai: Japan's Dreaded Military Police*, Sutton Publishing, Stroud, 1998
Lane, Arthur, *Lesser Gods, Greater Devils*, Lane Publishers, Stockport, 1993
Lane, Arthur, *Seventy Days to Hell*, Lane Publishers, Stockport, 2011
Lewis, Jonathan & Steele, Ben, *Hell in the Pacific*, Channel 4 Books, London, 2001
Lindsay, Oliver, *The Lasting Honour: The Fall of Hong Kong, 1941*, Hamish Hamilton, London, 1978
Lowry, Cecil, *Last Post over the Rising Sun*, Pen & Sword Books, Barnsley, 2018
Lowry, Cecil, *Frank Pantridge MC: Japanese Prisoner of War and Inventor of the Portable Defibrillator*, Pen & Sword Military, Barnsley, 2021
Lukacs, John D., *Escape from Davao: The Forgotten Story of the Most Daring Prison Break of the Pacific War*, Simon & Schuster, 2010
MaCarthy, Aidan, *A Doctor's War*, Robson Books, London 1979
Michno, Gregory F., *Death on the Hellships: Prisoners at Sea in the Pacific War*, Leo Cooper, Barnsley, 2001
Modder, Ralph, *The Singapore Chinese Massacre*, Horizon Books, Singapore, 2004
Moore, Aaron W., *Writing War: Soldiers Record the Japanese Empire*, Harvard College, 2013
Morris, John, *The Phoenix Cup*, The Cresset Press, London, 1947
Pearson, Judith, *Belly of the Beast*, New American Library, 2001
Pike, Francis, *Hirohito's War*, Bloomsbury, London, 2015
Priesman-Bogaardt, Louisa, *Dark Skies Over Paradise*, Trafford, Canada, 2005
Ramsay Silver, Lynette, *Sandakan: A Conspiracy of Silence*, Sally Milner Publishing, Binda, Australia, 1998
Rees, Laurence, *Horror in the East: The Brutal Struggle in Asia and the Pacific in WWII*, BBC Books, 2001
Russell (of Liverpool), Lord, *The Knights of Bushido: A Short History of Japanese War Crimes During World War II*, Skyhorse Publishing, London, 2008
Saburo, Ienaga, *The Pacific War 1931–1945*, Pantheon Books, New York, 1978
Sergeant, Harriet, *Shanghai*, Jonathan Cape, London, 1991
Shinozaki, Mamoru, *Syonan – My Story: The Japanese Occupation of Singapore*, Time Books, Kuala Lumpur, 1975
Starns, Penny, *Surviving Tenko: The Story of Margo Turner*, History Press, Stroud, 2010
Tanaka, Yuki, *Hidden Horrors: Japanese War Crimes in WWII*, Rowman & Littlefield, London, 1996
The Straits Times, 12 July 1946, '"Double Tenth" Men Hanged at Changi'
The Times of India, August 2014
Thompson, Peter & Macklin, Robert, *Kill the Tiger*, Hodder, Sydney, Australia, 2002
Thompson, Peter & Macklin, Robert, *Operation Rimau*, Hachette, Australia, 2015
Timperley, Harold, *Japan: A World Problem*, Robertson & Mullins, Melbourne, 1942
Tyrer, Nicola, *Sisters in Arms: British Army Nurses Tell Their Story*, Weidenfeld & Nicolson, London, 2008
van Kampen, Elizabeth & Lowry, Cecil, *Two Years of Tenko: Life as a 16 year old in a Japanese Prisoner of War camp 1943–1945*, self-published, London, 2015
Ward, Ian, *The Killer they Called a God*, Grenadier Press, Singapore, 1992

Wasserstein, Bernard, *War in Shanghai*, Profile Books, London, 1998
Widders, Robert, *Forged in Blood and Music*, Madra Beag Publishing, 2020
Wright-Nooth, George, *Prisoner of the Turnip Heads: Horror, Hunger and Humour in Hong Kong, 1941–45*, Cassel, 1994
Wyatt, John & Lowry, Cecil, *No Mercy from the Japanese*, Pen & Sword Military, Barnsley, 2008
www.archives.gov/files/iwg/japanese-war-crimes/introductory-essays.pdf
Zhou, Mei, *Elizabeth Choi: More than a War Heroine*, Landmark Books, 1995

Index